The Mary Rose Museum

THE STORY CONTINUES ...

Written by Anthony Burton.
The author has asserted his
moral rights.

Designed by Katie Beard.

Publication in this form
© Pitkin Publishing, 2014

Pitkin Publishing,
The History Press, The Mill,
Brimscombe Port, Stroud,
Gloucestershire, GL5 2QG
01453 883300

www.thehistorypress.co.uk

Printed in Hampshire,
Great Britain

ISBN 978 1 84165 478 2

1/14

Contents

Engineers turning the hull into the upright position in 1985

Timeline

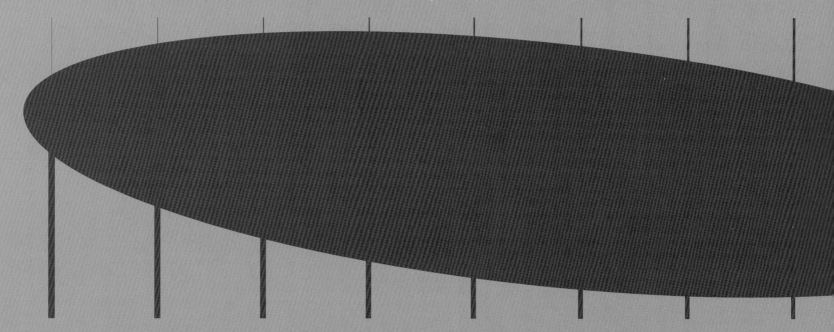

1510
The *Mary Rose* is constructed at Portsmouth

1511
The *Mary Rose* is commissioned

1512–14
England goes to war with France. The Lord Admiral, Sir Edward Howard, makes the *Mary Rose* his flagship and is involved in major actions off the Brittany coast. He is killed in action

1522–25
England is again at war with France and the *Mary Rose* takes part in the sacking of the Breton town of Morlaix. At the end of the war the ship is retired from service

1536–39
The *Mary Rose* is given a major refit

1543
Start of the third French war

19 July 1545
The *Mary Rose* capsized and sank during the Battle of the Solent

1823
John Deane and William Edwards recover four bronze guns, substantial parts of seven iron guns, several longbows and assorted shot from the wreck

2013
Spraying of the hull is completed. The Mary Rose Museum is opened to the public

2009
Work begins on the construction of the new Mary Rose Museum

2005
Divers recover the stem, a large anchor, and what is believed to be the ship's crest. A competition is held to select a design for a permanent museum to house both the *Mary Rose* and the artefacts. Architects are appointed for the interior and exterior

1984
An exhibition opens at Portsmouth dockyard for the first time. The hull and the artefacts are housed in separate buildings. The human remains of one individual are interred in the Anglican Cathedral in Portsmouth and a Requiem is held for the whole crew

1983
Construction of the Wemyss building over the dry dock to protect the hull

1982
The *Mary Rose* is lifted and brought back to dry dock in Portsmouth Naval Base. Conservation of the hull begins

1979
The Mary Rose Trust is formed with the aims of completely excavating the ship and raising her

1971
The *Mary Rose*'s hull is located. Margaret Rule, the team's archaeologist, makes her first dive on the site

1840
Attempts to further salvage the *Mary Rose* are again abandoned

1965
Alexander McKee heads a group of divers searching for the *Mary Rose* in the Solent

1970
McKee's team find the remains of an iron gun

1967
The Mary Rose (1967) Committee is formed following the discovery of an 1841 chart showing the location of the wreck, and prospection with sonar revealing a buried anomaly

Foreword

The opening of the new Mary Rose Museum is the start of another chapter in the extraordinary story of the *Mary Rose*. The boast frequently made is that King Henry VIII's favourite flagship and her incredible artefacts are this country's Pompeii – preserved in mud rather than fire and ash. Now that the new exhibition has been seen by so many visitors in a short time, there is a widespread understanding that the claim holds true.

The hull, still undergoing drying in the final conservation phase for the next two years, is the world's only 16th-century warship on display. It represents the ships that sailed out from Europe to make the 'Discoveries' to the Far East, to America, and then around the world. The *Mary Rose* is the first true warship of this nation's standing navy. All this is important to our history, but the greatest interest in the museum is created by the collection of artefacts from the ship, which provide the most stunning insight into life – and death – 500 years ago. From this great flagship that sank in action against the French, we can see the magnificent array of huge bronze and iron guns, together with their associated equipment. These are now positioned to show exactly where they were on that fateful day; and her gun deck is truly awe-inspiring. The fine (and unique) collection of longbows provides the only insight into the use of this significant weapon before it became redundant. The year 1545 was a time of pivotal change in naval warfare. The loss of the *Mary Rose* taught the nation a lesson that was proved well learnt 43 years later when fighting the Spanish Armada.

Even more fascinating is the insight the collection gives into everyday life at sea and ashore: the food and cooking, the clothes and footwear, jewellery and other personal possessions. We can see how the men lived, how they had suffered during their short lives from injury and ill health. The surgeon's equipment is eye-watering. By comparison, the carpenter's belongings look almost homely and utterly recognisable. Our visitors are leaving stunned, and moved, by the experience of 'meeting' the crew. The museum is dedicated to the men of the *Mary Rose,* and their individual marks are etched into the wooden exterior of the building.

Nothing has been easy about the *Mary Rose* project these last 40 years. Thousands of volunteers and staff have striven throughout by giving time, energy and money. Their early dreams are being fulfilled in this new exhibition. It has been a labour of love for us all; some have served continuously well over 30 years, but all have given everything they can to ensure success. This extraordinary new building has already gained great admiration – a veritable jewel box. The building of it,

The museum and its illustrious neighbour, HMS Victory

while we continued to conserve the *Mary Rose* inside in exacting conditions, has been nail-biting! It has been described as the most complex civil engineering project underway in Europe. But the work is complete, and on budget, thanks to the excellent teamwork of all our professional partners together with our dedicated staff.

We are already working on the next chapter, when we dismantle the hotbox required for conservation and remove it to expose the ship in its full glory without the appendages of drying apparatus. Then we can contemplate how much of the original timbers, such as cabins, bulkheads and ladders, can be reunited with the hull. So the future is most exciting, but our fundraising continues. With no government funding in this project throughout its history, we are here today through the generosity of trusts, businesses and individuals. Above all, it is the Heritage Lottery Fund that put its faith in the project and provided the bedrock of financial support. The income we receive from our visitors is vital to our sustainability, so we are grateful to everyone who comes to this museum and supports us in so many forms.

We trust that you will enjoy the museum for many years to come. Thank you for all your vital support.

John Lippiett

1

The End and the Beginning

The only contemporary illustration of the Mary Rose is from the Anthony Roll

THE SINKING

On 11 October 1982 the remains of the *Mary Rose* were lifted above the waters of the Solent, raised from the silt of the seabed where they had lain since the tragic sinking of 19 July 1545. To the estimated 60 million people who watched the event live on television, it marked the end of a remarkable story of salvage and rescue; for The Mary Rose Trust, it was the start of a new chapter in the history of the famous ship.

The Trust needed to provide a permanent home for the remains of the hull and the thousands of artefacts, from massive bronze guns to fragments of garments, which had been brought up from the wreck. It was to be another 31 years before that home would open its doors to the public, and it is largely the journey of those years that this book will tell. To understand the full story of the *Mary Rose*, these 31 years have to be seen in the context of the previous four centuries, and the story of the ship's creation.

Attempts at salvage had begun almost immediately after her sinking in 1545, when two Venetians were given the task of raising the ship. All they succeeded in doing, however, was breaking her foremast and rescuing most of the sails, though efforts continued to salvage the guns. A few more desultory attempts at salvage were made in the next few years and then

abandoned. Year by year, century by century, the starboard side of the ship settled ever deeper into the soft silt, while the port side steadily disintegrated.

REDISCOVERY

The next stage of the story began with a very different sort of accident. In 1818 a barn in Kent caught fire, threatening the lives of the horses tethered inside. One of the farmer's neighbours, a John Deane, came to the rescue. Unable to breathe normally in the dense smoke, Deane improvised, sticking the helmet from an old suit of armour on his head and pushing the tube from a fire pump inside it to provide fresh air. Inspired by this experience, John Deane's brother Charles later patented the idea of a helmet, fed with fresh air through a tube, for use in smoke-filled rooms. They then realised that the smoke helmet could be adapted as a diving helmet, and they began exploring underwater wrecks.

Positive identification of the wreck was possible because of the inscriptions cast into the barrels of bronze guns: the inscription on this gun lifted by The Mary Rose Trust, for example, carries Henry VIII's name, the Tudor rose and the date 1537

In 1836 John Deane and William Edwards were engaged to clear up the remains of the *Royal George*, which had sunk in the Solent in 1782. Approached by local fishermen to investigate an obstruction that snagged their nets, Deane dived the area and found much older remains. Amongst the wreckage was a 12ft-long bronze gun, described by Deane at the time as copper, which, significantly, carried the insignia 'HENRICVS VIII' cast into the barrel. There was only one ship of Henry VIII's navy that it could possibly belong to in that location: Deane and Edwards had found the *Mary Rose*. Over the next four years they salvaged all the visible remains. In 1840 they attempted to clear away the silt in what they believed was the hold of the ship by using explosive charges. Luckily for posterity, this had only a limited effect. Having recovered all they could, the site of the *Mary Rose* wreck was again abandoned.

The improvement of diving equipment and the development of scuba diving as a popular sport next brought an enthusiastic historian and amateur diver, Alexander McKee, into the hunt for the *Mary Rose*. McKee started diving to look for wrecks in the Solent in 1965. In 1966 a chart showing the position of the *Mary Rose* was found in the Royal Navy's Hydrographic Office. Remote prospection using sonar in early 1967 then revealed an anomaly within this area, prompting the formation

Divers preparing to go down to the Mary Rose *wreck during the 1970s*

of the Mary Rose (1967) Committee with the aims of finding, excavating, raising and preserving the remains of the ship and its contents. In addition to McKee, one of the founder members was archaeologist Margaret Rule. Rule was then engaged in a very different project – the excavation of a Roman palace at Fishbourne. She now had to add new skills to her professional qualifications: she had to learn to dive. In 1968 a lease to the seabed was obtained from the Crown Estates Commissioners, providing the only legal protection for the site.

UNDERWATER EXCAVATION

Further remote prospection and seabed searches revealed an iron gun in 1970. It was identified as coming from the *Mary Rose*, and the following year an even more exciting discovery was made. One of the divers, Percy Ackland, spotted, and more importantly recognised, that timbers poking up from the mud on the seabed were some of the frames of the ship.

Between 1971 and 1978 a series of targeted excavations were made to determine just how much of the hull remained intact. By the end of 1978 the team had proved that nearly half the ship lay buried in the silt, and the Committee was faced with several major decisions. Was the site important enough to warrant complete excavation and then raising the hull? And secondly: could the hull be raised safely? Two landmark meetings were held to answer these separate questions. The first was attended by archaeologists, ship historians, naval architects and museologists, and the second by naval architects, salvage consultants and structural engineers. As a result, the decision was made to excavate the hull with a view to raising it, provided it was deemed practcal following a detailed structural survey of the hull.

In January 1979 the charitable Mary Rose Trust was formed to raise funds and direct the ambitious project. HRH Prince Charles, who had first dived the site in 1975, agreed to be president, and an eminent board of trustees and an executive committee were formed. Margaret Rule was appointed archaeological director with overall responsibility for the excavation.

The difficulties the new team faced cannot be overestimated. The only precedent for lifting a

A well-preserved wheel from a gun carriage on the seabed

vessel of anything like this age was the raising of the 17th-century Swedish warship the *Vasa* in 1961. Over the years The Mary Rose Trust would collaborate closely with the Swedish experts, so that *Vasa* and the *Mary Rose* became sister ships, but no advice from the *Vasa* team could make the conditions for the underwater archaeology any easier. The divers worked in murky waters, with wretched visibility. The team included divers with many different talents. For instance one diver, Morrie Young, was a former shipwright whose practical experience was invaluable to the early dive team. Where no one could clearly see through the murk, Young was able to identify parts of the ship simply by the feel, based on his long experience.

Christopher Dobbs, now Head of Interpretation at The Mary Rose Trust, joined the team as a newly

Above left: The wheel on the support vessel immediately after recovery on an improvised support of ice cream cartons resting on a wooden pallet

Above right: One of the exciting discoveries was finding chests full of longbows in remarkably good condition

qualified archaeologist. He remembers those days with more than a little nostalgia. It was not the difficulties of the dive, Dobbs recalls, but his frustration at not being able to stay down there all the time, excavating the stunning objects. Divers were strictly limited to the amount they could stay submerged for safety reasons. Dobbs had to spend more time directing others than diving, and there were a lot of divers to direct. Between 1979 and 1982 there were over 27,000 dives on the wreck, involving around 500 volunteers who helped the regular team.

During the years of archaeological excavation on the *Mary Rose*, many new techniques had to be devised. Dobbs, for example, decided that some of the chests discovered underwater should be taken to the surface complete and unopened. This was not necessarily the

The hull of the Mary Rose being lifted from the Solent in October 1982

orthodox archaeological view of how things should be done, but proved to be valuable when it came to putting items on display and securely establishing which artefacts had originally belonged to which individual on board. The most important decision of all was how, or even if, to try and raise what remained of the ship, which consisted of part of the port side at the hold level and almost all of the starboard side apart from the stem post. The latter would be discovered and recovered at a later date.

RAISING THE SHIP

The Mary Rose Trust had been formed in 1979 and over the next four years it recovered more than 25,000 objects from the wreck. The Trust had to decide if the remains of the ship, weighing several hundred tonnes, could be lifted clear of the water without causing irreparable damage. Then, if the *Mary Rose* could be lifted, the Trust had to consider how they would raise the funds for both the salvage and the conservation, and where the hull and the artefacts would go to be put on display for the general public?

The controversial decision to lift was made, and an ingenious solution was found, which the proponents of the lift claimed would alleviate the risk of damage.

The hull being brought to the dry dock at Portsmouth, with HMS Victory *in the background*

This solution saw the hull attached by cables to a steel lifting frame while still resting on the seabed. The hull was then raised slightly, but still underwater, using hydraulic jacks attached to the legs of the lifting frame. Once it was clear of the seabed it could be transferred, again underwater, onto a steel cradle. The *Mary Rose*'s timbers were then fully supported, all the weight being taken by the cradle and the cables from the overhead frame, and it should have been quite safe to lift the vessel into the air and lower it onto a waiting barge.

The whole process was covered by live television, and aroused enormous interest. No one watching that day, either on site or in front of a television screen, will ever forget the heart-stopping moment when a pin attaching the lifting frame to one of the legs gave way, and there was a sudden lurch to the whole structure. Thankfully, everything else held and the lift was a complete success. Alexander McKee, who had been involved in the project from the start, described it as the most wonderful day of his life. For others, the occasion was one of rather mixed feelings. Archaeologist Alex Hildred certainly felt immense pride in what she and her colleagues had achieved, but it was touched with sadness. The *Mary Rose* had been their private domain for years and all that now remained on the seabed was a gaping hole.

A NEW HOME

The next great question, which had been long debated, was where the *Mary Rose* would find her new home. Various proposals were put forward for sites, including one near Southsea Castle, but the first choice went to Eastney at the eastern end of Portsea Island. When the time came, however, there was no possibility of the Eastney site being ready to take the ship, and the Ministry of Defence offered a temporary home in No. 3 Dock on Portsmouth's Naval Base. It was a moment of serendipity, for it meant that the *Mary Rose* was coming home to a site only yards from the spot where she was built. In the event, this temporary home was to prove to be her permanent resting place. It is altogether appropriate not just because of its location, but because the dock itself is historically important, part of another vital episode in the Portsmouth story.

Construction of the Wemyss building over the dry dock and the Mary Rose

Left: Alexander McKee and Margaret Rule proudly pose beside the newly raised hull

Below: The hull, still on its lifting cradle, installed in the dry dock

At the beginning of the 19th century, the naval architect and engineer Samuel Bentham had been employed by the Admiralty to make improvements to Portsmouth's royal dockyards. Bentham was an innovator and an ingenious man. When an old lady of his acquaintance, who loved playing cards, complained about her stiff hands, he invented a machine to shuffle the cards for her. It is no surprise, therefore, that when he reached Portsmouth he successfully brought in sweeping changes. Importantly, Bentham supervised the construction of a new dry dock, with stepped sides of massive stone blocks, and introduced another innovation, a steam engine, to pump out the water from the dock. The engine could also be used to power another new technology: the machines used to make blocks, essential parts of the rigging. The navy used thousands of these blocks: 922 of them for every 74-gun ship. Now they were to be mass-produced using machinery invented by Marc Brunel, father of the famous Isambard Kingdom Brunel. It was arguably the first modern mass-production factory.

The *Mary Rose* was thus in good company in her new home; an innovative ship in an innovative dockyard. It is important that she be seen not simply as a historic vessel in her own right, but also in the context of a historic dockyard that has developed over the centuries

Interior View "Mary Rose" looking East, T.Smith-nomber-.

and close to other iconic warships from a later age, HMS *Victory* and HMS *Warrior*.

There was now a difficult and sensitive engineering task to complete. The *Mary Rose* had been brought back on a barge and set in position on the bottom of the dry dock. One major construction project had to be put in hand straightaway: to provide the hull with a covered building so that essential conservation work could be carried out. This was provided by the Wemyss building, consisting of coated fabric stretched over an aluminium frame. The hull was still supported by the original cradle and was initially displayed as a wreck lying on its side. In 1985, the hull was turned upright and has been displayed ever since as a cutaway section of a ship – much like a giant, opened up dolls' house. This required a number of complex operations, during which as much of the lifting frame was removed as possible to give access and views of the ship. At the same time, former workshops in the

Above: Concept drawing for the initial display before the hull-turning operation

Left: Engineers and team announce that the Mary Rose has been successfully turned into the upright position

dockyard were made available for work on conserving artefacts that had already been brought to the surface, though later conservation work was to be carried out in the Chain Test House. The artefacts were not displayed next to the hull at this time, but in a separate building near the dockyard's visitor entrance.

Though they were to remain in use for over 30 years, The Mary Rose Trust always saw these buildings as temporary measures. They never lost sight of their main objective: to unite the ship and the artefacts in a purpose-built museum that would, in the Trust's own words, enable the '*Mary Rose* and her artefacts to tell their unique stories'. It was an ambitious idea that would require a large amount of money, and one of the key factors in getting the funding would be to persuade donors (especially the Heritage Lottery Fund, which was to provide more than half the money) that the *Mary Rose* was, and is, of immense significance.

A 21st-century painting by Geoff Hunt showing the Mary Rose under sail, based on the most up-to-date ideas on construction

2

The Mary Rose

It is easy nowadays to look at a vessel like the *Mary Rose* and see nothing more than just a very old ship. But if you had been alive in Tudor times, you would have been staring at the very latest thing in naval technology – the guided missile destroyer of its day.

The reign of Henry VIII marked a fundamental shift in the country's history: the medieval world was coming to an end and the Renaissance was just bursting into life. Similar dramatic changes can be seen in the *Mary Rose*; she was very much a ship of her time. The Tudor king is generally remembered for having six wives, for the dissolution of the monasteries and for starting the process that would turn England from a Catholic to a Protestant country. Henry VIII saw himself as the latest in a long line of warlike monarchs, but at the same time he loved innovation and wanted the latest and the best of everything. That desire to be up-to-date extended to building ships for his 'army by sea', the infant navy. Previously when the country had to fight a war at sea, merchant ships were commandeered and adapted for battle, which usually involved building structures in the bow and stern to provide a fighting platform for soldiers armed with longbows and arrows, or spears. Once peace returned, the temporary structures could be removed and the ships returned to trading. All this was about to change.

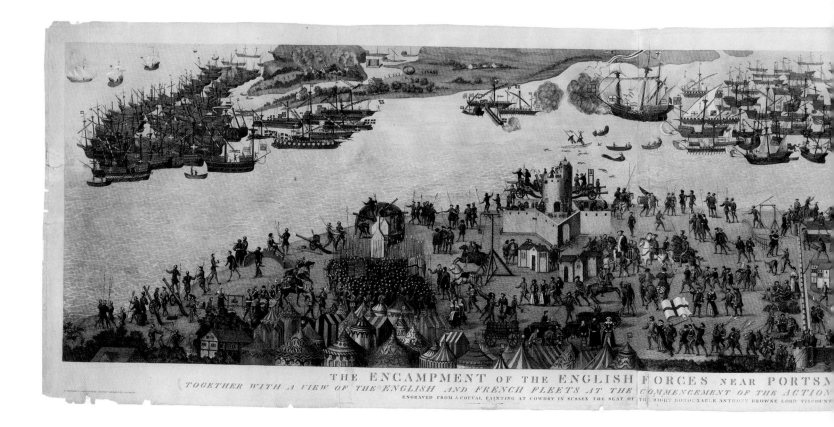

THE ENCAMPMENT OF THE ENGLISH FORCES NEAR PORTSM
TOGETHER WITH A VIEW OF THE ENGLISH AND FRENCH FLEETS AT THE COMMENCEMENT OF THE ACTION
ENGRAVED FROM A COEVAL PAINTING AT COWDRY IN SUSSEX THE SEAT OF THE RIGHT HONOURABLE ANTHONY BROWNE LORD VISCOUNT

The Cowdray engraving showing the ship's dramatic final scene, with the Mary Rose sinking, the English and French fleets, and Bembridge on the Isle of Wight in flames in the background

King Henry VIII decided that he wanted a fleet of ships built for war and for nothing else, and so began a ship-building programme early on in his reign. He had extra funds to spend in the 1530s, thanks to the money made by selling off monastic land, and he was thus able to pay for construction from his own purse. Portsmouth was then chosen as the main site for building the fleet. It was well defended by the stone Round Tower, replacing an earlier tower built by Henry V, and the Square Tower built in his father Henry VII's reign, which Henry VIII further fortified by adding Southsea Castle. The dockyard itself had been improved in 1495 by the construction of the first dry dock. So it was at Portsmouth, not in the dry dock but on the mudflats beside it, that construction of the *Mary Rose* began in 1510. Launched in 1511, she was to be the flagship of the country's first standing navy. This alone gives her a unique role in British naval history. In addition, as befitted the flagship of a new navy, the *Mary Rose* represented the very latest in ideas about naval architecture.

DESIGN

Traditionally, Europe had two quite distinct ship-building traditions. Northern ships, which included those of England, had clinker-built hulls constructed

N THEM ON THE XIXTH OF JULY MDXLV.

A man at work on the hull next to one of the small knees that supported the upper deck. Behind him can be seen the massive beams of the main and orlop decks

of overlapping planking, to which internal frames were added. It was the planking, not the frames, that gave the hull its strength. The southern tradition was quite different. Here, ships were carvel built. The shape of the hull was defined by a series of internal frames; planks were then added afterwards, abutting each other instead of overlapping. The hull had to be kept watertight by caulking, stuffing the spaces between the planks with oakum, which was then covered by pitch. Here the strength of the hull came from the frames, not the planks.

Carvel construction had one literally huge advantage over clinker building: it was possible to build far larger

vessels. With clinker building a point would have been reached when the hull of overlapping planks would start to collapse without the support of a strong frame. The carvel-built hull had no such problem, simply because the frame was put in place first. As it had a smooth outer surface, it would also move more easily through the water than the uneven hull of a clinker-built vessel. The *Mary Rose*, breaking with tradition in England, was carvel built.

The two traditions also differed in the types of sail that were used. In the northern clinker-built ships, a square rig had always been favoured, with the sail suspended from a spar at right angles to the mast and roughly at right angles to a line drawn from stem to stern. The archetypal clinker-built, square-rigged vessel would be the Viking long boat. In the south, they favoured a lateen sail. This was a triangular sail, hung from a spar running at an angle to the mast, still to be seen in the Arab dhow or the felucca of the Nile.

Each type of sail has its advantages and disadvantages. The *Mary Rose* enjoyed the best of both worlds: square rigged on the bowsprit and the fore and main masts, and lateen rigged on the mizzen and bonaventure mizzen masts at the stern.

She was a fine ship and, in a race against other vessels of the fleet in 1513, outran them all. We now

Divers watching as an iron gun is raised

know that more changes were made to the *Mary Rose* over the years. One of these involved fitting diagonal braces to strengthen her hull. This find came as a surprise to 20th-century archaeologists, as it had previously been thought that this type of bracing was introduced at a much later date.

WARFARE

During Henry VIII's reign, one of the principal tasks of a warship was to act as a troop carrier. If an enemy was engaged, the fight was at close range. The bowmen would shoot down on the enemy, the two ships would come alongside and the attackers would swarm onto the decks of the adversary for hand-to-hand fighting. The *Mary Rose* thus had the fore and after castles built permanently into her hull, and she was fitted with grappling hooks for engaging the enemy and a scythe to slice through the opponent's rigging. Several light guns, such as the swivel guns to be seen in the museum today, were fitted on the upper deck: numerous heavier guns would have made her top-heavy.

At some stage in her career, the *Mary Rose* went for a major refit. Routine repairs were carried out but there was also a far more important change made: she was fitted with gun ports, covered by tight-fitting

lids. These were square openings through which the muzzle of the guns could be thrust, and thanks to the lids they could be set low down in the ship while still remaining watertight. Because she was carvel built, cutting holes in the planking made no difference to the intrinsic strength of the *Mary Rose*'s hull, but would have affected the ship had she been clinker built in the traditional style. Although some clinker-built ships did have gun ports, they did not have the heavy, hinged lids that fitted snugly over the smooth hull, which could not have lain flat on a clinker-built hull. It was a fundamental change that would alter the whole nature of naval warfare for England and, ultimately, the whole of Europe.

Although the manufacture of guns had improved immensely throughout the 15th century, iron guns were still comparatively crude. Some were made by casting but they were liable to fracture: cast iron is very strong in compression, but not in tension. So the majority were forged using wrought iron, which has the opposite characteristics: strong in tension, weak in compression and better able to withstand the effect of expanding gases caused by the explosive charge. The very name 'gun barrel' gives a clue as to how they were formed. Long strips of iron, comparable to the staves of a barrel, were held together over a central core, and then iron hoops were heated and placed over the top, tightening their grip as they cooled, again as in barrel making. Iron guns were not entirely reliable and could be dangerous to use: James II of Scotland was killed in 1460 when such a cannon burst. Guns forged from wrought iron were recovered from the *Mary Rose* and are on show in the museum – at this time they were the most numerous guns in the fleet.

Where expense was no problem, a far more sophisticated technique was available. Bronze casting of a very high quality had been perfected in bell making (which gave rise to the apocryphal, and inaccurate, story that Henry VIII ordered bells from the monasteries to be melted down and recast as guns: the proportions of copper to tin in bell metal is different from that of gunmetal). Making a bronze gun was a highly sophisticated operation. A mould of the outside of the cannon was made, with all its decorative detail in place, together with a central core. The space in between was slowly and carefully filled with molten metal, an alloy that, in tests carried out on the *Mary Rose* guns, was generally 20 parts copper to one part tin. When the metal had solidified and was thoroughly cooled, the mould was broken open. Because a new mould had to be made for each casting, no two guns were ever quite the same. After casting, the core would

Left: An iron gun being lowered onto the deck of the diving support vessel Sleipner

Below left: A salvaged gun carriage being lowered into the dry dock for conservation treatment

be removed but the gun barrel still had to be bored to ensure the interior was smooth and even.

The bronze cannon found on the *Mary Rose* are simply magnificent, and their makers were rightly proud of them. Casting bronze guns had only recently been introduced to England, so they made it quite clear who had made these guns and where. The inscription on one of the guns reads:

ROBERT AND JOHN OWYN BRETHERYN BORNE IN THE CYTE OF LONDON THE SONNES OF AN INGLISSH MADE THYS BASTARD ANNO DNI 1537.

A 'bastard' was simply a type of gun that differed from the norm, and not derogatory. In 1514 the inventory of the *Mary Rose* included guns with far more alarming names: 'murderers' and even 'grete murderers'.

There was one other significant difference between the iron and the bronze guns. The former were breech loaded, so new explosive charges could be added without needing to move the whole gun. The latter guns were muzzle loaded, so the whole gun had to be hauled back inboard to reload after each firing.

Once fitted out, the ship was a powerful fighting machine with the biggest guns set down near the waterline to keep the vessel stable.

During the first French war of 1512–14, Admiral Sir Edward Howard was aboard the *Mary Rose* leading a fleet raiding the French coast when they encountered the enemy. He engaged the French flagship *Grand Louise* and reputedly used the guns on the *Mary Rose* to shoot away the French ship's main mast. But this was only to disable the vessel in order to bring the *Mary Rose* alongside for the English to grapple and board her. After her refit with heavier guns and covered gun ports, the *Mary Rose* could have used her firepower to sink enemy ships without the need to grapple and board them. War at sea would now be based on the idea of ships fighting each other at a distance, firing broadsides, rather than at close quarters. This was to remain the standard method of fighting for centuries.

Visitors to Portsmouth can see that exactly the same idea was used on Nelson's *Victory*; and that ships were still firing broadsides through gun ports in the 19th century, as the steam-powered ironclad HMS *Warrior* shows. The only difference being that on the *Warrior* they were rifled guns firing shells, not cannon lobbying round shot.

After the second French war of 1522–25, in which the *Mary Rose* was again involved, the vessel was laid up. She nevertheless went to sea again in the third French war, setting sail to join the Battle of the Solent

An iron gun in the foreground with a bronze gun behind it in The Mary Rose Museum: the differences between the wrought iron cannon and the cast bronze cannon are very obvious

on 19 July 1545. The French had landed troops on the Isle of Wight and it seems possible that the *Mary Rose* was being sent to help defend the harbour that day.

Exactly what happened will probably never be known, but we do know that, while manoeuvring, the *Mary Rose* suddenly heeled over, water flooded in through the gun ports that had been left open, and she sank. One of the standard procedures when close fighting was to cover the deck area with a canopy of netting to make boarding more difficult. In the event, it was to prove a death trap for those caught underneath the netting, who would have had little or no chance of surviving. Of the estimated 500 men on board, no more than 35 survived the tragedy.

A SIGNIFICANT SHIP

The *Mary Rose* marks a pivotal point in warship development: she incorporated all the latest ideas in ship design; she was the flagship of England's first standing navy; her weaponry changed the way wars at sea were fought, and marked the start of over three centuries of sailing warships with lidded gun ports. Moreover, when the *Mary Rose* was raised, researchers discovered still more unexpected evidence that she was the most advanced vessel of her day. This can be seen

by looking, for example, at the problems of navigation the *Mary Rose* would have faced: assessing the ship's position by finding out which direction she was travelling in and how fast, and plotting the results on a chart. It had always been assumed that the practice of mounting compasses on gimbals, so that the instrument would remain level despite the movement of the ship, had first been introduced no earlier than the 17th century. Yet there were three examples discovered on the ship.

Part of a ship's log was also discovered, a device which could have found a home without comment on *Victory* built more than two centuries later. On the *Mary Rose* it would have been the very latest thing. The log was a device used for measuring the ship's speed. A flat wooden float, not an actual log, was thrown overboard attached to a line wound round a reel. Once in the water, the log remained more or less stationary and, as the ship sailed away, the line was paid out for a fixed time measured by a sand glass. This gave a measure of the distance travelled in a set time, and so the

Far left: Margaret Rule and archaeologist Alex Hildred investigating a chest of longbows

Above left: The log reel just after it had been raised: part of the apparatus used to measure the ship's speed

Below left: Longbow arrows with the spacer in which they were placed, ready for use

speed of the ship could be calculated. Later, someone had the clever idea of knotting the line at regular intervals to make measurement simpler, which is why a speed of one nautical mile per hour is called one knot. Details such as speed are still entered in the ship's 'log' today, and the name logbook has come into general usage for recording data.

A reel and a number of sand glasses were recovered from the *Mary Rose*. The ship's navigator, armed with his compass reading and measured speed, would have used these to plot the ship's course. It is astonishing to discover how little some things have changed over the centuries: the dividers on display, for example, are exactly the same as those used by a modern navigator to measure distances on a chart.

A LEGACY

There is a very good case for stating that the *Mary Rose* is one of the most important ships ever built in Britain. But that is only a part of the story. When the ship sank she took with her some 500 men and their possessions, as well as all the different tools needed to keep a ship at sea, from navigation equipment to cooking ovens. These artefacts also have their own, often remarkable, stories to tell.

Among the recovered items were 139 complete yew longbows and over 3,500 arrows. The longbow has a special place in British history. It was thanks to this weapon and the skill of the archers that a small English force under Henry V was able to beat far superior numbers and phalanxes of armoured knights at Agincourt. The story is well known, yet no longbows in perfect condition had survived, or so it was thought until these were retrieved from the wreck of the *Mary Rose*. Previously, experts had had to make an estimate of what the draw force of a longbow would have been, and they came up with a figure of 90–100lb. The actor Robert Hardy, one of the country's leading authorities on the longbow, was one of the experts able to discover for themselves what the real figure might be. Given the length of the surviving arrows, which required a draw of 30in, it was possible to calculate that the draw force required was generally in the 90–100lb range as thought, but the largest bows required a massive 150–160lb draw. The archers were men of considerable strength and the longbow was a far more ferocious and powerful weapon than had ever been expected. Thanks to the discoveries in the *Mary Rose* shipwreck, a vital period of English history had to be rewritten. Museum visitors can now find out for themselves just how much strength is needed to fully pull one of these bows,

The imposing display of longbows and the chest they were found in

where a special exhibit has been created on the top floor at castle level: though visitors are not required to try and do more than draw half of the full 150lb force.

It is not only the larger artefacts which have changed our view of history that are important. Some small, apparently insignificant items also have their own stories to tell. Here is just one example. To fire a cannon the gunner has to apply a slow match – a slow-burning length of cord or twine – to the powder in the touchhole. Because this is accompanied by a flash of flame that could injure the gunner, however, the slow match is stuck in the forked end of a stick called a linstock. It doesn't necessarily need to be ornate, yet most of the linstocks recovered from the *Mary Rose* have elaborately carved ends with suitable motifs: a dragon's head to symbolise breathing fire or an aggressively clenched fist, for instance. The addition of the carving shows the pride of the gun crew in their work.

The vast number of items that were recovered, around 19,000, represent many different aspects of Tudor life, from religious beliefs to medical care. It is this rich variety that has led to the *Mary Rose* being compared to Pompeii, as representing a moment in time captured and held. Taken together, the historic ship and its contents represent a unique treasure that clearly deserved an exceptional museum.

Working on the concrete supports in the dry dock: the protective fabric cover for the ship's hull can be seen at the top left

3

Creating the Museum

FUNDING

During the early years of conservation, both the *Mary Rose*'s hull and some artefacts were on display to the public. But they were in separate buildings, so that it was very difficult to relate the found objects to the ship. To do so would require a new museum, where everything could be displayed under one roof. This was to be an expensive project: the costs were eventually estimated as £35 million, of which it was hoped £21 million would be provided by the Heritage Lottery Fund. To persuade funders to part with money on this scale, The Mary Rose Trust had to convince them that, with all the work that had already gone into conserving the ship and its artefacts, what was now needed was an appropriate permanent home. The Trust then needed to explain, and get approval for, their fundamental concept of how the ship and artefacts would be displayed, and what story they would tell.

The importance of the ship and its contents was clear to all who had worked on the *Mary Rose* project, and their views were reinforced by a number of independent experts who were more than ready to be quoted to stress the point. In terms of the story told, the Trust decided that this should essentially be the human one, to bring home to visitors that the men who died in the tragedy were real people, each of whom had

A section of the new museum's curved steel frame being delivered to the site

Left: *The Mary Rose Trust were keen to look at the best modern practices: here, staff are visiting the Ashmolean Museum in Oxford, which had a major, highly praised renovation project in 2009*

Below left: *New concrete foundations being laid outside the ship hall*

his own role in the life of the ship. The museum was not just to be about interesting the visitors, it would also be a lasting legacy to all those men who had sailed and died on the *Mary Rose*. The artefacts would be seen not simply as museum objects, but as things that were part of the everyday life of the men on board. In the words of the design brief, 'the museum must convey a sense of discovery, a sense of wonder and a feeling of stepping inside history.' The arguments were convincing and the story compelling; funding was secured.

CHALLENGES

Designing a new museum usually involves creating a building and then filling it with exhibits. On this project, the reverse was true. The main exhibit, the ship, was already present, fixed and immovable, and a museum had to be created around it. The Mary Rose Museum has thus been described as an 'inside out' project, in that the presence of the hull was the focus around which everything else had to be built; what was decided about the interior would be a determining factor on the design of the exterior.

That was only a part of the challenge. When the hull had been set in place in the dry dock in 1982, it had been protected from the elements by the

The completed museum

overshadow HMS *Victory*. It also had to take its place in a historic dockyard that already had a number of iconic buildings. Any new building had to be at least as dignified as its predecessors and complement them, rather than compete against them. To describe the task as challenging would be a gross understatement.

EXTERIOR ARCHITECTURE

Architects were invited to tender for the job and offer their designs. In the event, the contract was awarded to a team of two architecture firms acting in a consortium: Wilkinson Eyre Architects would be responsible for designing the exterior and Pringle Brandon Perkins+Will for the interior.

The final exterior design of the ship hall and exhibition area is striking, based on elliptical forms that mirror the curved shape of the old ship's hull. The final design does not simply copy the shape of a 16th-century warship, but it does have a strong maritime look, rather as if it might be the template for a sleek, modern luxury yacht. As well as being aesthetically pleasing, the shape gives the visitor an idea of its function. As architect Chris Wilkinson explained, although the building only had a 'supporting role' for the treasures inside, it still had to 'project the Museum and its remarkable collection to the

1983 Wemyss building, a structure that had allowed conservators and archaeologists to work whilst also giving some access to the public. The hull had needed to be contained within a closed environment inside the ship hall, in which atmospheric conditions could be closely controlled and, during the latter stages of conservation, it would need to be boxed in whilst being sprayed and then dried. It was now imperative that this environment should be maintained intact throughout the construction period of the new museum.

Work on the site continued in all weathers

There was a further demanding constraint. The dry dock in which the *Mary Rose* sits is a Grade 1 Scheduled Ancient Monument, and so nothing could be done to the dock that would cause irreversible damage. Account also had to be taken of the fact that the museum would have a famous neighbour: the new building was not to

outside world'. There was also a very practical reason for choosing this design. By following the lines of the hull, the exterior minimises the interior space that needs to be kept under controlled conditions. It was designed as a steel frame to which red cedar timber cladding would then be added, appropriately in much the same way as the carvel-built boat would have been constructed. The analogy with the *Mary Rose* inside the structure is enhanced by the window openings, simple squares and rectangles cut in the cladding, strongly reminiscent of gun ports. The red cedar was then stained black, following a long vernacular tradition for boathouses of all sizes. The design also gives other suggestions of what lies inside, including a balcony very reminiscent of a modern ship's bridge.

Two simple rectangular pavilions were designed for either side: one to hold the museum reception area, shop and cafe; the other for an education centre and control plant. The completed building looks magnificent with its beautifully clean and simple lines. That apparent simplicity, however, conceals a much more complex story.

The original design saw the museum resting on four immense piles outside the dry dock, enabling the museum to be effectively suspended inside the dock. This involved substantial complexity and a

Work on erecting steelwork at the east end: it is curving round the cover protecting the hull

large amount of structural steel, and so the successful contractor, Warings, a subsidiary of Bouygues UK, put forward an alternative that instead supported much of the load from the dock itself using a combination of pad and strip foundations. This had the advantage of significant cost-saving and avoided the risks associated with piling alongside the ancient dock. This proposal didn't change the outward appearance of the museum and the only structural alteration that had to be made to the dock itself was the removal of coping stones. These were all numbered and stored so that, in the highly unlikely circumstance of the museum being moved, the dock could be returned to its original condition.

Erecting prefabricated steel frames and then adding external cladding is a commonplace building technique these days, but the vast majority of structures built in this way are foursquare, not elliptical. In these conventional designs construction is simple: standard off-the-shelf steel elements can be used and, because they all meet each other at right angles, erection is straightforward. This museum building was very different. Here it seemed that steels came in a bewildering variety of shapes and sizes, and that the joints where they met also came in a variety of different angles, so many elements had to be individually tailored to do the job. The framework,

Left: *A mock-up of the cladding for the outside of the museum*

Far left: *The east end ready to receive its cladding*

when completed, looked like an elaborate metal cat's cradle, and constructing it proved to be one of the most difficult problems of the whole build. Altogether, nearly 500 tonnes of steel were used in the process.

As the work progressed, the Wemyss building was steadily dismantled without compromising the integrity of the closed environmental box – no easy matter when scaffolders are swarming all over the place, looking for somewhere to place the next pole. But, thanks to the co-operation of everyone involved, the steel structure was completed while conservation work on the ship continued uninterrupted. The building was now ready to receive its outer cladding of red cedar planks that would then be stained black.

The overall effect of the building is strikingly dramatic, but it is also worth taking time to search out some very attractive small features on the exterior structure. At various points the planks are inscribed with copies of the different signs that were used by the mostly illiterate crew of the *Mary Rose* to mark their personal property. More conventionally written letters are also inscribed to spell out the names of benefactors of the modern-day building.

What the visitor does not see from the outside is the hugely complex system installed to maintain the conditions in the museum, especially those

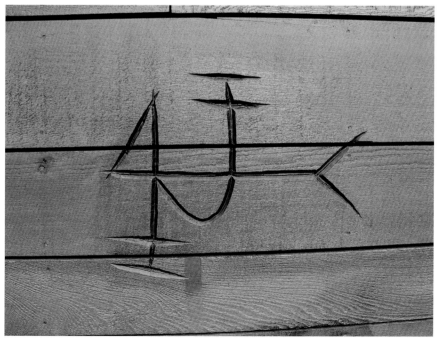

Left: *Marks belonging to the crew of the* Mary Rose

Far left: *Workers constructing the museum's roof*

used to control temperature and humidity. Right underneath the building, down in the dry dock, is a labyrinth of pipes and cables. Installing these was not straightforward. Normally, to fasten pipework in place all you would have to do is drill a few holes, install some brackets and the job would be done. Not here, however, in a listed structure. There could be no drilling into the stones so everything had to be placed on freestanding supports. Statistics can be boring, but these are so startling they are worth quoting. Tucked away in the space left between the museum building and the dock, and spreading out through the museum itself, are 400 kilometres of electric cabling, 1,500 metres of steel piping, and 800 metres of copper piping. Originally, the plant house that controlled the systems within the Wemyss building was inside the dry dock area. During the building of the new museum this had to be removed, and so a complex operation had to be put in place to provide new control systems to take over the essential work.

Throughout the build, decisions had to be taken on what was financially possible and what was not. It was absolutely essential to keep within budget. Quite early on, for example, one of the original design elements had to be radically changed. The original plan had called for a concrete roof, which would have

a high thermal mass. In effect, this meant that it would store thermal energy and help to maintain an even temperature inside the building regardless of the weather outside. It was soon realised, however, that the extra steel required to support the huge weight of a concrete roof was too expensive, so the Trust turned instead to specialists Kalzip who constructed a much lighter roof from aluminium and zinc, whilst still retaining similar thermal properties. This new roof was provided in prefabricated sections for easy assembly.

The budget-monitoring process continued throughout the build, and a number of cherished ideas had to be abandoned along the way, but the result was that the museum came in on budget. Not many large building projects can boast that achievement.

Above: Work on the balcony that will provide a unique view of HMS Victory and the docks

Left: Staining the cedar wood cladding under the sweeping curve of the balcony

INTERIOR ARCHITECTURE

The design of the interior was very much a collaborative effort between the Trust and the architects, and for Chris Brandon of Pringle Brandon Perkins+Will, it was the perfect opportunity to combine his two passions, as he is also a maritime archaeologist. Everyone agreed that walking into the museum had to be a very special experience. The visitors should feel as if they were walking into history, entering the *Mary Rose* as she was in the moments before she sank.

The museum was thus divided into three floors, each one coinciding with one or more of the decks of the ship: the lowest – the hold and orlop deck above it – above that the main deck, and then the castle deck. To one side, there is the surviving starboard hull, rising to the full height of the building. On the opposite side is a mirror image of the starboard side, a space that allows the artefacts to be seen in context. So, for example, a gun will have its muzzle pointing through a gun port in the virtual hull, directly opposite the actual gun port on the starboard side, while barrels and rope are displayed down in the hold, as if at the bottom of the ship.

The reception and entrance to the museum is a bright, airy space with a desk, shop and cafe. But once the visitor moves into the elliptical building, everything changes. It is quite dark, reflecting the dark spaces

A display case with the panel opened up to reveal the complicated system that controls humidity and temperature

Left: *Maintaining conditions of temperature and humidity within the display areas requires a complex system of pipes, all tucked away out of the sight of visitors*

Below left: *Part of the piped system of the under-floor heating in the entrance pavilion*

between the decks of the old ship. There is no natural light and the artificial lighting is kept to a minimum, allowing attention to be focused on the objects themselves.

The central area down which visitors first walk is sloped, just like the real deck opposite. This creates an impression of being on a not-quite-steady surface, an effect heightened by faint creaking noises of moving timbers played over speakers. Down on the lower deck, the ground floor, the effect is even more realistic as the groans of the wood are joined by the noise of lapping waves. The creation of the atmosphere of actually being on board a ship has proved so successful that several visitors have asked the staff how they manage to make the building move.

The illusion itself is heightened by the way in which the floors have been arranged. On the lower two floors, corresponding to the areas below deck on the ship, the gap between floor and ceiling is considerably less than on the top floor, which in turn represents the airy upper deck. Although the main building does contain offices and facilities for the staff, they are not obvious to the visitor; entrances being through dark doors set into dark walls. Nothing takes away from the magical atmosphere of the museum.

As with the exterior architecture, there were specific problems brought about by the site itself that had to be solved inside. The museum has a lot to offer, but it is not huge, so there are limits to how many people can visit at any one time. It therefore made sense to plan the interior so that visitors could follow a fixed route with a coherent narrative from the beginning to the end. At the building's heart, and indeed the heart of the route, is the ship itself, which can be viewed from all three levels. Around this, the artefacts have been arranged to tell the story of the vessel and the men who lived in it and died in it, partly in the mirror image of the starboard side and partly in display cases at each end.

In most museums you enter at ground level and wander up through the different floors or, as in the case of the famous Guggenheim Museum in Bilbao,

Above left: Construction work underway on the interior: building the west end of the main deck

Above right: The maintenance area in the constricted space down in the dry dock

you are whisked up to the top and then walk back down a spiral. At The Mary Rose Museum the entrance is at ground level from the outside, as is normal, but because the ship sits at the bottom of the dry dock on the site, visitors are actually coming in halfway up the building and ship. A way therefore had to be found to lead visitors on a comfortable and logical journey of discovery, without constantly climbing up and down stairs. This was largely achieved by making gentle transitions between the three different levels; a route has been carefully planned to ensure that visitors can fully take in the whole story of the *Mary Rose* in a logical progression – and they never have to walk up any stairs unless they want to, only down.

Many decisions had to be taken on how to display the ship and its treasures, and one of these was how far

Preparing the secondary collection artefact store

of the museum they pass a wall displaying a film of an underwater scene, in which various objects are seen falling down towards the seabed while other, lighter objects are drifting slowly up. The objects illustrate the things that belonged to the men of the ship; a poignant reminder that this museum is also recording a tragedy in which almost 500 men died. Like the overture to an opera, it sets the mood for the story that will soon unfold as the visitor walks round.

THE ROUTE THROUGH THE MUSEUM

Entering on the ground floor, the visit starts at an entrance presided over by the man who ordered the ship and witnessed its end, in the shape of a life-size model of Henry VIII, seen in his robust prime. Inside the first main exhibition area there is then a short explanatory film and a large illuminated display, a greatly enlarged projection of the Cowdray engraving, showing the Battle of the Solent. This was based on an original painting, commissioned by Sir Anthony Browne, Master of the King's Horse, who appears in a prominent position in the work. He is appropriately mounted on a handsome, prancing white horse, immediately behind the king. The original hung with four other

to make use of modern audio-visual techniques. These are obviously a valuable aid to understanding, but there are problems too. It was clear to the exhibition designers, Land Design Studio, that the stars of the show were the physical remains of the ship and its artefacts, and it was through them that the past would be brought alive. Anything else that was added needed to play a secondary role and never detract from the exhibits themselves. It might be tempting, when even a smartphone has sophisticated computer graphics that were once reserved for Hollywood blockbusters, to go for spectacular audio-visual effects, but that was not the route the museum followed. Instead, audio-visual is used subtly to make quite specific points where the technique helps to set the scene and tell the story. So, for example, as visitors first walk into the darkened area

French Fleet

Installing the large interactive display based on the Cowdray engraving, and the completed Cowdray display

discover details from the big picture. Back-lit vignettes give extra information and relate to objects displayed in the museum. Altogether, it provides a wonderful context for the story of the ship and a spectacular way to present the drama of the sinking.

THE MAIN DECKS

The route leads the visitor into the display space opposite the main deck of the ship. Here in the darkened central space the ship's hull can be seen to one side and its mirror image on the other. This is actually part of an immense structure, 34 metres long and rising to the full height of the hull, and contains objects placed in context, as they were found within the ship. At the far end of the gallery there are smaller display cases containing the possessions and objects associated with three of the men who would have lived and worked on this deck: the master carpenter, the master gunner and the surgeon. These are the cases designed to help with the vital role of telling the human story.

On this level, the guns are the most obvious artefacts displayed opposite the ship, together with all the things the crew would have needed to use them, such as the equipment used to load them and the ammunition. The latter were not just what are popularly known as

paintings of the king's campaigns in Sir Anthony's home, Cowdray House in West Sussex, but was destroyed in a catastrophic fire in 1793. Fortunately, it had been copied and a number of coloured engravings survive.

Engraved by James Basire of London, the version seen in the museum may well have been worked on by his apprentice who was to go on to greatness: William Blake. It is a remarkable image that shows a bird's eye view of the scene, which would of course have been impossible for the artist to achieve other than in his own imagination. In spite of that, comparison with modern aerial photographs has shown that it is remarkably accurate. The view shows the French fleet on the left with the English on the right, and between them, right in the centre of the picture, are the top masts of the *Mary Rose* sinking beneath the waves. A forlorn figure waves from the crow's nest, while bodies float around him. Touch-screens enable visitors to

Left and above: One of a pair of giant cauldrons being lowered into the brick furnace in the galley display on the lower deck level

The completed display area on the upper deck, showing officers' sea chests and their contents

cannon balls, but more properly are called shot. There was also canister shot, designed to break apart on reaching the target, throwing its lethal contents in a spray of flint fragments.

THE LOWER DECKS

A similar pattern is repeated as the route leads down, via steps or a lift, to the floor below, or the lower decks. A gallery and display cases can be seen at each end. This area provides access to both the storage (orlop) deck and the hold, full of barrels, ropes and cable, and the characters represented here are the purser and the cook. This area also housed the galley where the food was prepared for the officers and crew. It may come as

Above left: Work on preparing the 'virtual' upper deck, which would be a mirror image of the starboard side of the ship

Above right: Officers and gentlemen ate off pewter plates: this one embossed with the coat of arms of Viscount Lisle

a surprise to find brick-built structures on board a ship, but it was essential to provide a safe area in which a fire could be lit without setting the entire wooden ship ablaze. There were originally two ovens side by side on the *Mary Rose*, each with a giant copper cauldron set above a brick firebox. Both have been recovered: one is intact, looking just as it would have done when in use, and the other is in the chaotic state in which it was discovered on the seabed, the cauldron battered and misshapen, the fire bricks lying around it.

This area also contains the archaeology gallery that deals with everything from underwater exploration to conservation of salvaged artefacts and environmental remains, and it contains some human remains, discussed later (pp. 99–105).

Left: *The view from the glass-sided lift joining all three floors*

Far left: *The western end of the museum showing the Bridge Balcony at night*

THE UPPER DECKS

The final part of the tour takes the visitor up two floors to the top floor of the museum, to be level with the castle decks of the ship. This is where life is made easy for visitors: they can walk up two flights of stairs if they want to, but there is also a very special alternative. A glass-sided lift joins all the three floors: running up past the stern of the *Mary Rose*, it gives an uninterrupted view of the whole length of the hull.

The upper deck was home to the officers and gentlemen, and displays emphasise the differences in living standards with the lower decks, contrasting the pewter plates of this level with the crude wooden bowls used by the men in the bowels of the ship. Unlike the ordinary seamen with few possessions, the officers had imposing personal chests containing a rich variety of articles. This upper deck is also the

area associated with the soldiers who sailed on that day, and displays concentrate on the weapons they used from the officers' swords to the longbows and hand-held firearms. From here, stairs lead back down to the final gallery before the exit. This tells the story of the search, excavation and recovery, and includes film clips of the original live televised broadcast of the lifting of the hull.

THE VISION

The dream of The Mary Rose Trust from the start was to have an iconic building that would take its place next to the maritime icon that is HMS *Victory* as part of the rich heritage of the historic dockyard. Even more importantly, the building had to be a showcase for the preserved hull and the thousands of artefacts that would eventually be on display. Making these elements available in a stable condition, and arranging and displaying them so that they told a coherent and very human story, was always at the heart of the whole concept of creating the museum. But artefacts that have been on the seabed for centuries could not just be popped into cases to be admired, nor could ancient timbers be seen in their full glory until the archaeologists and conservators had done their work.

Conservation and Construction

4

Once the *Mary Rose* had been raised and taken to the dry dock, the work of conservation could begin. Some of the timbers, such as decking planks and cabin partitions, had been removed to make the lift easier, leaving what remained of the main hull all in one piece. This included virtually all of the starboard side and part of the after castle, but not the stem, which (as already mentioned) was discovered and raised later, and is being conserved separately. The deck planks have now been replaced, but the cabins will be added later.

A team was assembled to carry out the conservation work that included a young scientist, Mark Jones, who had recently received his doctorate for work on marine anti-fouling. Now, 30 years later, he is Head of Collections as Professor Jones.

PRESERVING THE WOOD

The team's first job was to clear away by hand any sediment still trapped between the inner and outer planking of the hull, and then begin the process of preserving the wood. The basics are simply expressed: wet wood is unstable, but once dried the wood is stable, provided it is kept in the right environmental conditions. Of course, to get from the one state to the other is far more complex than such a simple statement

The start of conservation work on the hull: spraying with water in the dry dock in 1983 as the Wemyss building is erected around the ship

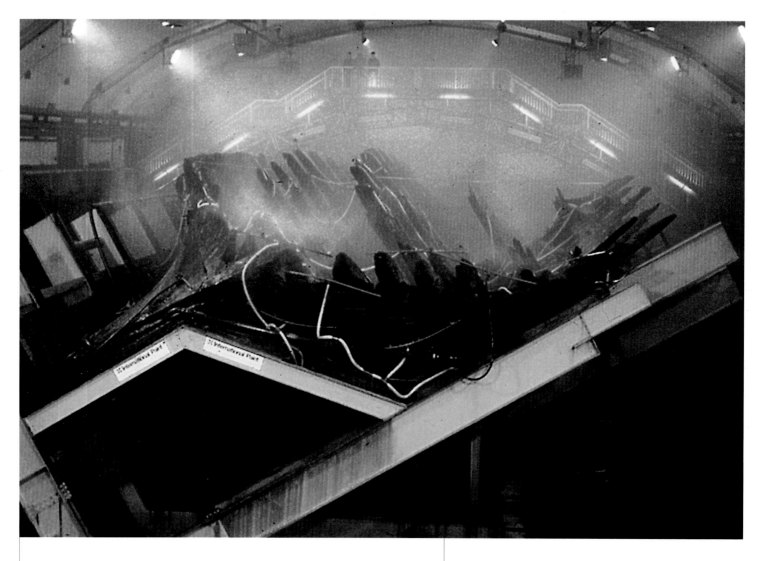

suggests. For a start, the timbers were not just saturated with water, they were saturated with salt water. And over the years, two little creatures, the isopod *Limnoria lignorum* and the ship-worm *Teredo navalis*, had bored their way into the timbers. A standard treatment would have been to immerse the timbers in a huge tank for treatment, but that was impractical for a number of

Above and right: The ship before the jacking operation to turn her upright

reasons: given the sheer size of the hull it would have been very expensive, and it could not have been put on public view. Instead, a much slower method lasting many years had to be used: spraying the hull with very cold water, between 2°C and 5°C. The salt water was gradually flushed out and the cold prevented fungal and bacterial infection. The spraying had another

Left and right: *Operating the jacks attached to the cradle*

advantage: the public could see the ship while the work was in progress – and the fees the public paid were a valuable, and much needed, source of revenue.

Those who visited the vessel during this time often have very fond memories of what seemed to be quite a romantic scene, with the ship emerging from the mist like some spectral vessel. It was a good deal less romantic for those who had to work on the ship under these conditions, as the sprays could only be turned off for an hour at a time – constraints similar to those encountered during the diving phase of the operation.

Once the cold water had done its job, the hull was still left saturated with water. The answer was not to dry it out immediately, because the water-filled wood would simply have collapsed if the moisture was removed, leaving nothing but air to take its place, and the timbers would have cracked and shrunk to about half their original size. Advice was taken from the conservators on the Swedish ship *Vasa* who had faced a similar problem, and it was decided to follow their example and use polyethylene glycol (PEG) to stabilise the wood. Apart from being a well-established compound for preserving wood, PEG has another valuable property. In theory it can be removed from wood so that if, at some time in the future, conservators

In the early years, the visitors were in the same damp, chilly atmosphere as the ship

Sprays could be turned off for short periods to enable archaeologists and conservators to work

have found a better substitute, they will be able to use it instead. Making only reversible changes is an important part of the conservation creed.

The prefix 'poly' in polyethylene glycol indicates that this is a polymer, a chemical that has a repeating pattern of atoms as part of its structure. In PEG, there is an arrangement of carbon, hydrogen and oxygen, which can be repeated over and over again to make ever bigger molecules, in the way that links can be fastened together to make chains. The more links there are in the polymer chain, the bigger the molecules will be and the more they will weigh. This makes it very versatile, as solutions of different molecular weight can be used at appropriate stages of the process. The *Mary Rose* process started with PEG of a comparatively low molecular weight in dilute solution, and worked up to much higher molecular weight and more concentrated solutions. Again the ideal method of treatment, soaking in a giant tub, had to give way to the longer, slower process of spraying.

Environmental conditions during the PEG spraying were now very different from what they had been earlier. Due to the process there was now a temperature of 30°C, though there was still 97 per cent humidity. It was imperative that these conditions were maintained, and the sprays were never allowed to stay off for

Once the PEG spraying had started, the visitor galleries had to be glazed and air-conditioned

more than an hour at a time. An alarm system linked to an emergency telephone alerted a member of the conservation team if anything was amiss. The team member then had to see to the problem at once – even if the emergency happened at three in the morning, which was not unknown.

Because of the extreme conditions, working inside the hull was limited to an hour at a time and was extraordinarily difficult. It proved more problematical than expected to reach the required levels of PEG in the outer layers, but the end was reached at last in April 2013 after 19 years of spraying with the preservative. One of the team, when asked what it was like when the spraying finally stopped, summed it up in a single word: 'Heaven!'

DRYING THE WOOD

The next stage of the conservation process, begun in 2013, is drying the wood by blowing environmentally controlled air through a complex system of textile ducts arranged around the ship's structure. These were set in place and supported by stainless steel rods and anodised aluminium tracks while the PEG spraying was still in progress – a difficult and very unpleasant task. The pattern of laying the ducts and directing the flow of

air around the hull was determined by careful scientific analysis under the direction of Dr Glenn McConnachie who, tragically, died before the work was completed. The process has to be slow and gentle and is expected to continue until 2016. No one can be entirely sure, however, as there are no exact precedents to go on. Small samples of wood are taken regularly, rather in the way that a cheesemaker will bore out a sample from a cheese. These are then weighed, dried and then reweighed to determine the water content to check how far and how fast the drying process is proceeding.

The drying process is carried out in a giant hotbox that had to be kept in place even after the new museum opened. A series of windows have been created in the box to allow visitors to see the hull from the museum walkways, and the harsh working lights have been replaced by more subtle, dramatic lighting. This was supplied by DHA Lighting, an organisation that knows a great deal about theatrical lighting, having worked on many successful productions such as *Les Miserables*. Lighting a huge area such as this is as much an art as lighting any drama: highlighting what needs to be emphasised and providing background illumination without being obtrusive.

To complement the architectural scheme, the museum also uses a rolling light on the *Mary Rose*,

While the wood was being sprayed anyone working in the hull had to wear full protective clothing

a lighting pattern that constantly changes but only slowly. Visitors may not even be consciously aware of it, unless they stand for a long time looking carefully at the hull, but the slight changes give an effect of the play of natural light constantly shifting over time. It all adds to the sense of actually being aboard a moving ship rather than in a static museum.

Tests to check on the drying process are not the only ones being carried out using core samples. Some are taken to the Harwell Research Centre in Oxfordshire for investigation using the Diamond Synchrotron. This is one of the country's latest and most advanced scientific facilities, opened in 2007 at a cost of £263 million. An electron gun produces subatomic particles that are accelerated almost up to the speed of light. This produces light beams of immense intensity, 10 billion times brighter than the light of the sun. It enables the scientists to peer deep into the structure of the wood. They look specifically for the iron content, where the wood has been in contact with metal objects such as bolts, and for sulphur, which has the potential to turn into sulphuric acid that could cause severe damage. Thanks to the synchrotron, the *Mary Rose*'s conservators and scientists can compare sulphur at the surface of the wood with the content at its heart.

Monitoring of the hull will continue, even after the drying process has come to an end.

CONSTRUCTING THE SHIP

Although the ducting will have to remain in place until the conservators are happy that drying is complete, visitors still have a far better view of the hull than was possible when it was only seen through a misty spray. The main elements of the structure can be clearly observed and the first impression is of remarkable complexity. This is quite accurate: a wooden ship such as this is indeed complex.

Oak predominates and, long before construction started, suitable trees would have been earmarked for felling – some chosen because they were straight and suitable for planking, others because they were curved and suitable for cutting into shaped ribs, braces and knees. Ships such as this consumed a vast amount of timber. A near contemporary vessel, the *Great Michael*, built in Scotland in 1506, was described in an early history of maritime architecture as 'having wasted all the woods in Fife which were waste wood'. It has been estimated that the oaks from something like 36 acres (14.5 hectares) of woodland would have been cut down just to construct the *Mary Rose*.

The view of the hull from the gallery with ducting in place for drying out the timbers

Once the timber was available, the master shipwright would have needed to provide accurate shapes for the main frames that would define the shape of the hull. He worked using very large compasses – big brothers to the ones found in school geometry sets today – which is why the timber used for all curved sections was known as 'compass timber'. Thin wooden templates, known as moulds, would then have been made from the drawings and used to check that the timbers had been cut to the correct curvature. Traditionally, this shaping was done using an adze, an implement like a long-handled axe, except that the blade was set at right angles to the handle compared to an axe blade. This meant that each swing of the blade cut out a curved chip of wood. The indentations left by the adze are a familiar sight on old wooden ships timbers.

Construction would have begun by laying down the keel, at the very bottom of the hull. This was made of elm fore and aft, and oak midships, as experience had shown that elm, unlike other timbers, becomes virtually indestructible when waterlogged. The keel consisted of three sections, joined together by overlapping scarfe joints. Stem and sternposts would then have been added together with the keelson that lies on top of the floors above the keel. The sternpost was straight, which allowed the massive rudder to be

attached. This reached all the way up to deck level, where the tiller would be connected. The cross-section of the tiller is round, but the after end has been squared off to fit into a square hole cut into the rudder, where it would have been pinned into place. It is perhaps surprising to find such a large vessel steered by a tiller instead of a wheel, but the steering wheel had yet to be invented!

Floor timbers were attached to the keel using oak pegs, known as treenails (pronounced *trenn-els*). Then, the carefully shaped ribs would have been put in place. Beams were built to join the two sides of the hull, to support the deck planking and, at the same time, give greater strength to the frame. Ribs and beams would have been joined by knees, which are basically like overgrown versions of brackets used to hold up shelves, all made out of wood. This is where oak was particularly suitable. For in parkland or at the edges of a wood, the branches emerge more or less horizontally from the trunk, so a skilled carpenter is able to cut out a knee in which the grain of the wood runs true. Support would be given by knees placed below the beams, known as 'hanging knees', with 'rising knees' above the beams.

Once the frame was completed, with extra timbers added between the ribs, the planking could be fitted

and the whole hull made watertight. After the hull was completed, the rest of the ship would have been fitted out, adding everything from cabins to masts. Some of the timbers that can now be seen date from the *Mary Rose*'s later refit.

There are several distinguishing features to the hull. It is of a kind known as tumble-home, and the curve of the hull is such that the vessel is broader in the beam than she is at the level of the upper deck. One big advantage of the shape is that it allows extra space for big guns to be mounted at the widest part of the vessel.

Those who have had the opportunity to work inside the *Mary Rose*'s hull have even today been struck by the quality of the craftsmanship. Many of the details may have been new at the time she was built, but the

Above: An illustration from a book by the Tudor shipwright Matthew Baker, showing Tudor shipwrights at work laying out the lines of a ship

Left: Another of Baker's illustrations, showing a man carrying a knee. It also shows the tumble-home shape of the hull as seen in the Mary Rose

job of constructing a large wooden ship was based on centuries of tradition and the knowledge of the master shipwrights. These were men who guarded their knowledge carefully – they were masters of techniques that were aptly known at the time as 'mysteries'. Indeed, there are no written records of shipbuilding until 1586 when Matthew Baker, son of a master shipwright from Henry VIII's reign, produced his *Fragments of Ancient Shipwrightry*, which included a number of detailed drawings as seen here. Before that the 'mysteries' were passed on by word of mouth and by practical experience gained through long apprenticeships.

The *Mary Rose* today is a magnificent tribute to both the master shipwrights and the craftsmen who worked with them, and the archaeologists and conservators who have done so much to preserve her.

5

From Seabed to Showcase

The skeleton of the
carpenter's dog, nicknamed
'Hatch' by pupils at Whitgift
School, Croydon

UNDERWATER

The work of preparation for museum display began even before any artefacts were brought to the surface. An essential part of archaeology, whether as part of a conventional dig on land or, as here, underwater, is the careful recording of each object *in situ*. On some occasions it was easy to identify belongings and place them with accuracy because of associated artefacts, or because the cabins they belonged to were still intact.

The skeleton of the carpenter, for instance, was found together with carpentry tools. Many of these tools were instantly recognisable and would be familiar to a modern-day carpenter, including planes, mallets and whetstones for sharpening the tools. Rather less familiar was a delicately carved whetstone holder. One surprise did await the excavators however. Along with the tools, the skeleton of a dog was found near the entrance to the carpenter's cabin. We may never know whether the animal was kept purely as a pet or, more likely, for the more practical job of killing the ship's rats.

Another important collection found was connected with the surgeon. One of the essentials on a warship, where injuries often required drastic treatment without the benefit of anaesthetic, was the ability to carry out an amputation as quickly as possible to prevent the patient dying from shock rather than from his wounds.

The first surgeons were therefore barber-surgeons, employed on the principle that the man who could handle a razor neatly and rapidly to remove whiskers was capable of managing a scalpel with equal dexterity. The surgeon on the *Mary Rose* was far too important to take on such a menial task as hair cutting though. Indeed he had to be very versatile, combining the duties, in modern-day terms, of GP, surgeon and pharmacist. He had an array of ointments and concoctions stored in jars and canisters, ready prepared bandages, and some dangerous-looking implements, including a trepanning tool for drilling holes in the skull. The artefacts found even hint towards the morality of the crew, as the surgeon's instruments included a syringe used for treating venereal disease. Most remarkable of all, the surgeon's traditional velvet cap was also found, preserved for years in the silt of the seabed, and is now a fascinating part of the current display.

Other artefacts were not so easily attributed, but the position in which they were found in relation to the wreck was carefully recorded. Every single one of the 19,000 or so objects that were brought up had to be given a number and all available information noted. The list identified where its original resting place was in relation to the section of the ship in which it was found. Without this careful work carried

Clockwise from top: The urethral syringe from the surgeon's chest, very little different in design from a modern-day syringe

The crew were plagued by head lice, and as the surgeon had no effective chemical treatment, the men used nit combs. This one is made out of boxwood

A simple stool that could have been knocked up by the ship's carpenter

One of the ship's compasses

out below the waves, it would have been impossible for archaeologists to later make sense of all the finds and accurately position them within the mirror image of the hull. This was vital because of the sheer number and incredible variety of objects that were retrieved. There were many finds that were part of the ship herself, such as the blocks and other parts of the rigging, ropes, cables and fragments of sail cloth. Then there were all the elements associated with the fighting ship: the cannon, handguns, pikes, longbows and the equipment that went with them. Also retrieved were barrels for storage, some of which contained the remains of animal carcasses, butchered cattle and pork, together with baskets full of fish and even one basket with plum stones.

The most poignant items that came up from the sea were the personal possessions; reminders that, although this was a warship, only a fraction of its life was spent in actual battle conditions. The rest of the time everyday life continued. We know from the artefacts that there was opportunity for relaxation as well as work: the men played games, including backgammon, while the officers were entertained by an array of musical instruments. Two fiddles and bows, three tabor pipes, a tabor and a still shawm were all retrieved. Tabor and pipe were a combination played

79

More personal items included articles of clothing and shoes. There was even a reminder that although the king had broken religious ties with Rome, England was still a Catholic country, and some crew members still kept their paternoster beads. There is also evidence that, despite the fact the men and their officers had a certain amount of enjoyable leisure time, they also had to deal with some unpleasant stowaways that came along for the ride: eighty nit combs were found among the men's possessions. These were only a few of many examples where discoveries on the *Mary Rose* provided exciting new material in many different disciplines, not just maritime history.

There was obviously a great deal of excitement when interesting and unexpected new discoveries were made, but a lot of the items were far more mundane. It made no difference, however, to the work of conservation. Every one of the 19,000 artefacts is precious in its own way, and each one has to receive a treatment appropriate to its condition and the material of which it is made. While there might be a good deal of satisfaction in treating an officer's sword found in remarkably good condition, there were many repetitive tasks too. There is probably not a great deal of obvious pleasure to be had from cleaning up literally

by one musician: the tabor a drum played with one hand; the pipe, a simple tuned whistle, held in the other hand. The still shawm, or douçaine, is a woodwind instrument with a double reed, the forerunner of the modern oboe, with a considerably harsher tone than the oboe but softer than the usual shawm. Its discovery caused huge interest in the music world because, although it had been referred to in documents, it was the only example of this particular type of instrument that is known to have survived to the present day. Visitors to the museum can hear a recording of replicas of these instruments being played.

Paternoster beads: a reminder that, in spite of the break with Rome, England remained a Catholic country

Left: *A bronze gun being lifted onto the deck of the salvage vessel. Unlike iron, bronze does not suffer from concretion*

Below left: *The linstocks used to hold the slow matches for firing the guns were carved with suitably ferocious heads*

hundreds of old bricks, yet even these have their appeal to the specialist. Today, bricks are machine-made, coming out in uniform size, colour and texture. This was not the case in the 16th century, when every brick was made by hand and firing temperatures were variable. As a result, the bricks are all slightly different, ranging in colour from a salmon pink to a deeper red. They too have a story to tell about the technology of Tudor England.

ON THE SURFACE

From the start, the divers and archaeologists worked closely with the conservators to ensure the objects that had been retrieved with so much effort and hard work did not deteriorate once they were brought to the surface. It would have been impossible, given the huge number of objects emerging from the silt, to begin conservation on all of them at once. The first step was to place objects in what is known as 'passive storage': storage that did no more than keep the objects as nearly as possible in the same condition as they were in when they were first found. Various materials required different initial treatment and protection against numerous types of attack; everything from fungi to chemical reactions had to be considered.

Above: *Some of the 1,200 cast iron shot for the guns recovered from the wreck*

Left: *An anchor, one of the larger iron objects recovered, receiving an initial cleaning*

Treatments varied from the purely chemical to the biological. Bone and ivory, for example, had to have all the salt solution removed from them to prevent it crystallising. Small wooden objects could simply be sealed into polythene bags to keep in the moisture, and a similar treatment was used for leather and textiles. Larger timbers were kept in open water tanks. Other treatments seem quite bizarre. It is a little surprising to find that one effective way of getting rid of organisms that attack wood is to use the common pond snail. The creatures gobble up the unwanted organisms without damaging the wood. A more conventional form of protection against fungi and microbes was to store wooden objects at very low temperatures. Metal objects presented quite different problems. Once exposed to the air, iron, copper and copper alloys were liable to oxidise, and reactions were possible from chlorides that had penetrated the surface, having formed from the common salt of seawater. To prevent damage, iron artefacts were therefore kept in a sodium hydroxide solution. Other metal artefacts made of lead alloys and pewter required different treatments, from electrolysis to soaking in acid.

As with the conservation of the hull, the presence of iron and sulphur in wooden artefacts had the potential to cause major problems. Iron is often found, for example, where the metal was originally attached to a wooden object, such as in a wooden-handled knife or dagger. The iron will have corroded but could still leave traces in the wood. The sulphur would have originated as a result of biological activity while the object was on the seabed. As long as an object was covered in silt and salt water there was very little oxygen available and so no reactions occurred. But once an object was brought to the surface and exposed to the air, it was possible for a chemical reaction to produce corrosive acid. There were two types of treatments used in these instances. One was to remove the iron content, the other to neutralise the chemicals that could cause corrosion.

The Trust's scientists have developed their own pioneering techniques as well as relying on the experience of conservators at other museums. Recent successful experiments have been made using strontium carbonate as a neutralising agent,

WOOD

The wooden object is one of the largest on show, a gun carriage that supported one of the iron guns. The first essential process was to clear away concretion resulting from the corrosion of the iron fittings. The gun and its carriage were then soaked in an alkaline solution until it was possible to separate the carriage from the gun. It was then necessary to work out the actual state of the wood – how much water it contained, and how far any damage had penetrated. The treatment of the gun carriage wood was similar to the method used on the hull, except that it was possible to soak the different elements of the whole carriage in a bath of PEG rather than just spraying it. This sped up the process so that it was completed in about two years, compared to the 19 years spent spraying PEG on the hull.

The drying process, however, was entirely different from that used on the hull. The first stage was to freeze the gun carriage down to a temperature of -30°C (the PEG actually prevents any damage occurring down to -40°C). This temperature ensured that all the remaining water turned into ice. Simply heating up the ice would have been no help, as it would just have melted back to water again before it could be driven off as steam. However, there is a way round the problem. Most people know that water boils at 100°C, but this is only true at

which can remain in the wood after treatment without causing any damage. Often the larger artefacts require prolonged treatments: two of the tanks contain a remarkably well-preserved anchor and the wooden bore of the ship's bilge pump, and they will need to remain in treatment for years to come before they are considered to be completely stable. Conservation can never be hurried.

The conservators now work in the former Chain Test House, a spacious iron-framed building that, like the dry dock, is also a listed structure. Their workplace needs to be spacious as, apart from holding bulky objects awaiting treatment, it is also home to the treatment tanks and the specialist equipment needed for conservation. The best way to understand the processes involved is to follow the history of three of the museum's items on display: one of wood, one of iron and the other of leather.

Above: Due to concretion caused by corrosion of the iron, the shape of this wrought iron gunpowder chamber is scarcely recognisable

Left: A conserved anchor being placed in its display setting

Far left: *The dismembered parts of wooden gun carriages placed in a tank ready for conservation*

Left: *A wooden gun carriage being moved*

Below left: *Gun carriages in the freeze-drying chamber*

sea level. If the atmospheric pressure is reduced the boiling point comes down. That is why you can't make a decent cup of tea on Everest: the air pressure is so low that water boils at a temperature of just 68°C. Reducing pressure is thus the key to removing the ice. If the air pressure is reduced, almost to the point of creating a complete vacuum, and a small amount of heat is added, then the ice will sublimate, which is the scientific way of saying that it goes straight from a solid to a vapour without passing through the liquid stage at all. This is the technique that was used on the gun carriage, pumping out the air to create a vacuum in the treatment chamber.

After treatment the wood of the gun carriage was preserved, but after nearly five centuries mostly spent underwater, it no longer has the structural strength to support heavy iron guns. Yet for display purposes, it was obviously far better to have the gun and its carriage united to show how they appeared when in use. The answer was to support the gun itself on a steel frame, leaving a gap of just 5mm between the frame and the carriage. Although the steel frame is visible if you look hard enough, it is not obtrusive, and the overall effect is to show the two elements together, a Tudor gun on a Tudor carriage. It is not quite the complete unit they would originally have been, as it was not possible to support the gunpowder chambers.

IRON

The iron object we have chosen for our comparison is a hand-held gun that, unlike the mighty cannon, was not forged but made out of cast iron in a foundry. It is an important find, for although a few larger guns had been cast, it was not common practice. Yet 20 cast hand guns were recorded for the *Mary Rose*, suggesting a shift in technology at this time.

Iron objects on the seabed made a very comfortable resting place for all kinds of marine creatures, especially various types of shellfish such as barnacles. Over the centuries the metal became covered with an accretion that set like concrete. This was not a problem with the bronze cannon because the copper in the alloy is toxic to these creatures, which is why in later years wooden sailing ships had the bottoms of their hulls covered by

Above: Concreted iron gun as lifted, before the gun was separated from its carriage

Left: An iron gun on display in the museum. Mounted on its carriage: the supporting steel frame is scarcely noticeable

copper sheathing. The accretion that formed on the iron was not altogether bad news for the conservators, as it acted like a protective shield, but it also created a problem. The accretion may have formed specifically on the iron, but it would also have surrounded anything else that happened to fall on top of or alongside the metal object. In addition, when looking at a typical concreted object there is no clue as to what might lie underneath: almost the only things visible would be fragments of seashells. One answer was to radiograph the object, and the Royal Navy made their non-destructive testing facilities available for the job at much reduced rates.

Once it was known exactly what lay under the accretion, the work of removing the hard mass could get underway. This did not require any complicated machinery, just a hammer and, as a last resort, a chisel and a great deal of care. Once the weapon was revealed it was discovered that it was still loaded, and the conservator found the wadding and the tampion, used to ram it home, together with the gunpowder that, amazingly, was still dry. The ammunition consisted of iron dice shot – tiny metal cubes. Originally, it would have been attached to a wooden stock, and the gun would have been fired with the stock tucked under the arm and the barrel resting on a rail. This was a scatter gun, the shot spreading out very quickly. It was

The iron hand-held gun that was found to be still loaded with small iron dice

a weapon that could be used at close range against enemy personnel and didn't require careful aim to inflict a lot of damage.

Once the concrete-like accretion had been removed, the iron had to be treated in a sodium-based solution to remove chloride and sulphide compounds, followed by washing. Once this process was complete, the gun was coated with an acrylic resin to protect it from further contamination. It was now ready to be put on display with the rest of the ship's armament.

LEATHER

The third selected item is a leather shoe. The early conservation processes consisted of washing for a period of time, cleaning-up the shoe, immersing it in PEG or Bavon, and then freeze-drying it.

One of the things that the conservators wanted was to identify the animal(s) that had provided the hide from which different leather items would have been made. To do this they turned to experts in Northampton, the traditional centre of the British shoe industry. With most samples of leather they were able to define the hide as being cow, calf, sheep, pig or deer simply by examining the grain of the leather. However one small sample, which may not even have been part of a shoe, baffled even the leather experts. Eventually, they came up with the answer: the item was probably made from the tanned hide of a dog. They were also able to advise on the best way to preserve the suppleness of the leather by treating with a fat-liquor compound Bavon 520S.

Perhaps the most remarkable thing about the range of shoes found was not just that they were so well preserved, but that the different techniques used in their manufacture are fundamentally the same as those used to make modern-day shoes, the only difference being that the shoes on the *Mary Rose* would have been made by hand, not by machine.

All of these three wood, iron and leather items are now on display in the museum, each having a specific place in the overall story.

Above: *Leather ankle boots that still had their laces*

Right: *Among the other leather objects discovered was this ornate bottle*

BACKGAMMON SET

1 The Master Carpenter owned this 'tables' set [1], a game which developed into backgammon.

The lighter coloured triangles are yew; the darker triangles are spruce or larch. The board could be folded in half and the rebates for the hinges can still be seen. But the iron hinges have rusted away during the years the wreck was underwater.

2 Only some of the backgammon counters [2] survived. Originally there were 15 dark and 15 light ones made of poplar. You can see that the edges have been [...] they feel [...]

IN THE MUSEUM

The first museum for the *Mary Rose* collection was by the entrance to the dockyard, a long way from where the ship was being sprayed. The new museum gave the opportunity to combine the displays of ship and artefacts in one building. Part of the vision was to show many more objects than had been displayed before and the team started by developing the narrative – the ideas for the stories that would be told in the new museum. Then they needed to choose the objects to display and how to display them. Some were in storage and the Trust's scientists first had to conserve them. Having chosen them, it was not just a matter of popping them into cases bought off the shelf. Like everything else involving conservation of the *Mary Rose* and her artefacts, arrangements had to be made for long-term preservation within the displays.

During the planning stage, the overall pattern of displays had been agreed and suitable display cases then had to be ordered. The specialists that won the contract to provide these was the German company

Above: Parts of the ship's rigging have been preserved. This double block is in astonishingly good condition

Left: A backgammon set found in the carpenter's cabin on the main deck

Reier, who had an international reputation for fine craftsmanship having manufactured cases for many world-class museums from the Kremlin in Moscow to the Victoria & Albert in London. The Mary Rose Trust, however, presented them with new problems: how to supply cases, some of them very large indeed, in which atmospheric conditions could be very tightly controlled to within +/-1°C and 4 per cent humidity. It involved a great deal of experimentation and close co-operation with the Trust's own experts, who made a number of journeys over to Germany. In the end, a complex air-conditioning system had to be installed in each case, hidden away behind panels such as the ones in which the AV screens were mounted. The only hint the visitor gets to indicate this complexity is the monitor visible in each case. This constantly measures temperature and humidity, and feeds the information back to the central computer in the control rooms, through which the whole system is managed.

Meanwhile, work began on creating the displays. Curators selected the items that should be put on show, together with the in-house designer Rosie Smith, who checked the items chosen would work as a display. Other members of this museum team worked on the mounts and designs. Several important decisions were taken. The first was that it should always be made clear

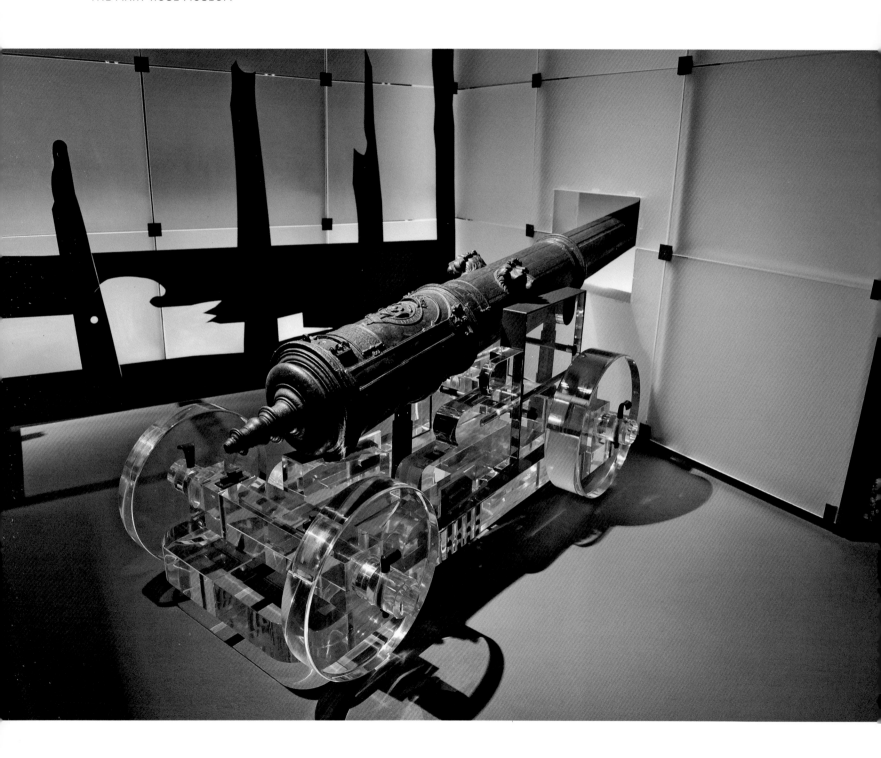

to the public if anything had been added to the artefact since it had been conserved. An obvious example would be an arrow, which, devoid of its flight and point, looks just like a thin, round stick. The choice was made that there would have to be something extra to show how it would have looked in its original condition. In this and all other examples, it was decided to use opaque frosted acrylic for additions to the original object. Sometimes the acrylic additions were small, and often so unobtrusive that visitors are scarcely aware of them; in others cases they are large and complex. For example the bronze cannon seen here is mounted on acrylic, which acts both as a support and as a representation of the original carriage. This means that visitors can be absolutely confident that anything on display in a case that isn't obviously plastic is indeed a genuine object salvaged from the sea, even if in some cases it looks too perfect for that to be true.

Above: The displays were designed with the help of scale models of cases and artefacts; this mock-up was for the carpenter's display

Left: A magnificent bronze gun on its new acrylic mount

Another decision concerned how the exhibits should be mounted in the cases. With such a huge diversity of objects, some of which were quite robust and others very fragile, each item had to be considered individually. It was agreed that the best way of achieving the perfect results would be to make all the mounts in-house. This was a huge operation as each one had to be individually designed and then manufactured out of clear acrylic. The mount was precisely cut with a laser and, if necessary, curved by heat treatment. Some objects, such as the fragile books, had to be completely supported for protection: others could simply be free standing. Each display case then had to have its contents carefully arranged for maximum effect and to tell a story. Once the artefacts had been selected for each case, scale models were made of both the cases and the objects to go in them. At first these were simple cardboard pieces that could be moved around easily until the best arrangement had been agreed on. Then, full-size mock-ups of the cases were made and laid out using the real objects. This meant that when the actual cases arrived the work of filling them went far more smoothly than even the most optimistic had hoped. But before that day arrived there were still other jobs to complete.

Although the artefacts are intrinsically interesting, visitors need to know something about them. Writing

captions is a tricky balancing act between not providing enough information so that people are left with too many questions, and providing so much detail that the effect is daunting and no one can be bothered to read it all. Here that balance has been achieved: there are descriptive panels putting the objects in context as well as shorter captions describing the individual artefacts. There are further aids to understanding the artefacts: handling collections, interactives, computer games and AVs developed with Spiral Productions. Short films have been made with actors in costume – some of them museum staff – seen going about doing the everyday tasks of the ship's crew, using copies of the objects on display to demonstrate how they were used. Even the carpenter's dog gets a part.

The artefacts are not just objects to put on display in a museum: they are invaluable archaeological finds that needed to be carefully recorded. Each item was given a unique identifying number from the moment it was recovered and available information – where it was discovered, what it was made of and so on – recorded and later added to as more information emerged during conservation. They had to be photographed, often at several stages during the process, and, in most cases, drawn. A record sheet was made for each item, giving a description of its state when conservation was

The completed mirror image gallery on the main deck with the upper deck visible above

completed. That way, any future researchers would know, for example, whether a chip out of the rim of a bowl was there when it was brought back to the surface or was the result of a later accident.

Once the objects were ready and the cases had been planned, the question of lighting the displays had to be addressed. Some artefacts have to be protected from strong light – probably everyone is aware of what happens to some fabrics in sunlight as they ruefully decide that their faded curtains need replacing. The final decision was to ring the inside of each case with tiny fibre-optic lights that can be individually adjusted, so that some artefacts are more brightly lit than others depending on the need and display.

The displays represent a team effort involving interpretation, conservation, recording, designing, arranging and captioning. Underlying everything, however, is the need to ensure that all the items are preserved in pristine condition. Each display case is actually a complex piece of technology, with heat, humidity and lighting levels all carefully controlled and monitored. If visitors are totally unaware of this then the cases are a success. As one of the team remarked: the best mount is an invisible mount. So too, the best technology does its work silently and unobserved.

6

The Crew

It has always been an important part of The Mary Rose Trust's philosophy to ensure that all the human remains recovered from the wreck are treated with dignity, respect and high standards of care. The Human Remains Advisory Committee (HRAC) was set up to ensure that this policy was carried through, whether it was advising on what might be displayed in the museum and how, or authorising scientific investigations by outside researchers. It is recognised that these remains are more than mere artefacts for investigation and display: they were once parts of the living bodies of those who worked on the ship. It was agreed that there should be a single burial in Portsmouth Cathedral to represent them all, much as the tomb of the Unknown Soldier does for the dead of a later war. At the interment in 1984, a special Requiem service was held for the whole crew.

Altogether, the remains of 179 individuals have been identified, of which 92 have been classified as 'fairly complete skeletons' (FCS). In practise, the emphasis is often rather more shaded towards the 'fairly' part of the classification than the 'complete'; most have less than a third of their bones and only 24 have skulls that can be matched to bodies. Other remains are too scant to make identification possible. As with all artefacts brought up from the sea, their location in

The completed figure of an archer on display in the museum next to his skeleton

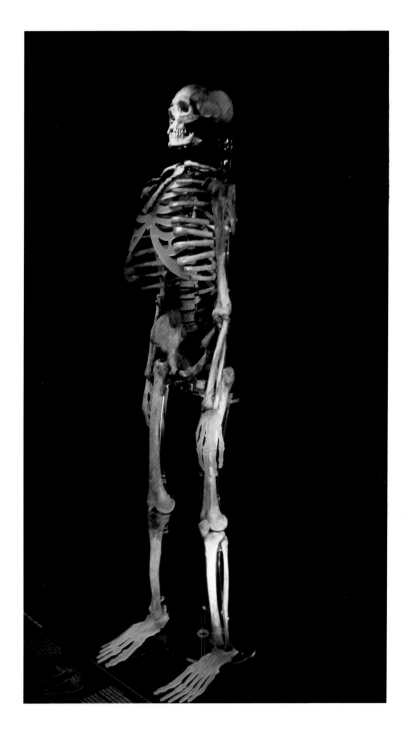

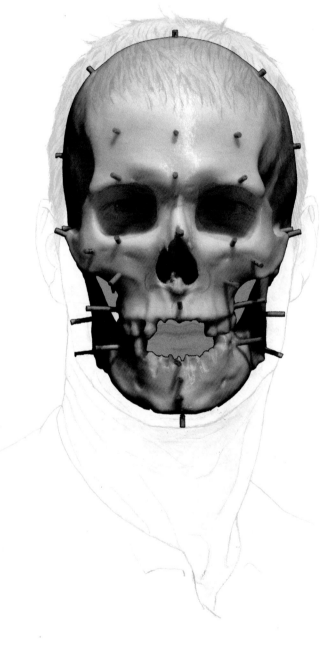

relation to the ship was carefully recorded, offering the first hint of the role an individual might have had in the crew. On a few occasions, the skeletons were more or less complete, sometimes found contained in items of clothing or alongside artefacts. Elsewhere, large numbers of bones were found together and were lifted to the surface as a unit, where the daunting task of sorting them into individuals could begin. A start could be made based on a simple fact of human anatomy: our bodies are symmetrical. This means that if two thighbones, for example, were found that were of the same size and shape they could be placed as belonging to one individual. Then, if a pelvis was discovered and those bones fitted perfectly into the sockets, then another piece could be added to the skeleton. So work proceeded until, in a few cases, individuals could be laid out with the bones of torso, limbs and skull. There were two important questions the Trust now had to answer: how much would the skeletons tell us about who the individuals were and what they did? And, if some sort of identification was possible, should the bones be put on display? The good condition of some of the human remains, combined with a study of their bones and the fact that artefacts were found alongside them, has enabled archaeologists to give tentative occupations to at least ten members of the crew.

Far left: The skeleton of a man identified as an archer on display

Left: Reconstructing facial features: the pegs on a 3D replica of the skull indicate the depth of flesh over the bone. The outline of the head has been shaded in

THE ARCHER

The most complete skeleton, numbered FCS7, was of a big, powerful man standing 5ft 10in tall. Expert investigation showed an interesting feature in both of his shoulder blades, a phenomenon known medically as 'bilateral os acromiale'. In lay terms, this means the bit of the shoulder blade that extends over the joint is separated from the rest of the bone by cartilage in the young, but gradually fuses over the years to form a complete bone – the condition occurs when this fusion fails to happen. One possible reason is that the joint had been put under a lot of strain during the formative years. Testing on men who had been practising archery for a long time showed that they frequently suffered from painful shoulder joints but not this condition. However, those tested had all started the sport comparatively late in life. In Tudor England, it was a requirement that boys should be taught archery from a very young age, so the hypothesis is that the strain had an effect before the bone had a chance to fuse together in puberty. This is only a theory: no one has ever been able to look for this condition in a modern boy who had practised archery every day throughout his youth, so no direct comparisons are available.

It was decided to do a full-scale reconstruction of the archer as a museum exhibit. A very obvious

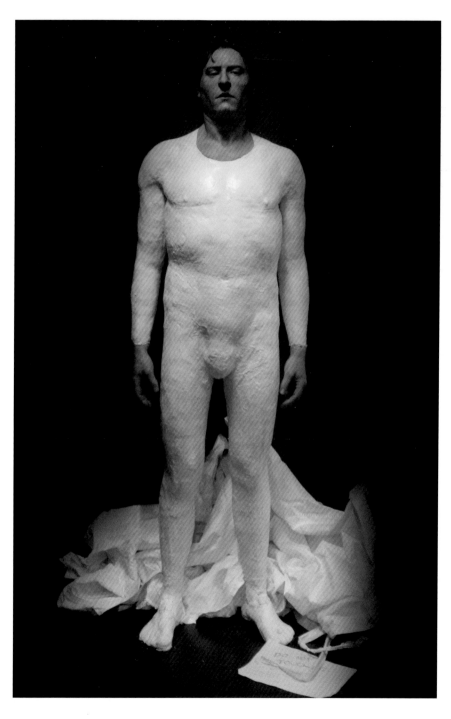

requirement for an accurate, lifelike model was for him to have a face, and not just any face, but one that would, as accurately as possible, resemble his appearance when he was alive. Reconstructing faces from skulls is a technology frequently used in forensic science, and has proved invaluable in many police investigations. Measurements made with living volunteers have provided a set of figures for the normal amount of flesh covering each part of the skull for people of either sex and at different ages. FCS7 was a man in his twenties so, using the available data for a European male of this age group, work could begin. Pegs, lightly attached to the replica skull, indicated the depth of flesh at different points. This was translated into a computer image and used to build up the different features. Some details, such as the colour of eyes and hair, have to be guessed at, but the face that emerged was of a very rugged individual. He was given a suitably muscular body and then appropriate clothing, and was then ready for display. The question still to be decided, however, was whether or not his skeleton should also be put on show.

Before any decisions were taken, the Trust carried out a trial display of human remains together with reconstructions, and visitors were asked for their responses. The survey showed that over 90 per cent of people were in favour of showing the bones. The accepted principal governing the display of human remains requires that mounts should not impact on the bones, so the archer's bones are mounted on an acrylic frame. There is no doubt that seeing the two together – the actual skeleton and the reconstructed figure – does have real value in emphasising that the *Mary Rose* story is a very human one.

FCS7 is the only skeleton that has been given a full reconstruction in the museum, but other remains also had stories to tell, stories that have brought out interesting facts about the individuals who have been given a place in the museum.

Left: A reconstruction of the muscular body of the archer

Right: The jewelled cross and silver ring that were found in the chest believed to have belonged to the master gunner

THE GUNNER

Another fairly complete skeleton studied was FCS16. Aged between 30 and 40, and 5ft 5¾in tall, he was found on the main deck by a ladder leading to the main deck. He was wearing a leather jerkin with stitch-holes in the form of the cross of St George on both front portions and centrally on the back. These are seen on gunners in contemporary illustrations. The top of a gunpowder flask was attached to his jerkin, and a thimble-ring used to sew thick material like that of gunpowder cartridges was found within his jerkin. He had degenerative changes to his spine, sacrum and

sternum, possibly as a result of lifting heavy objects. Moving the guns, loading them and particularly lifting the heavy gunpowder chambers from the iron guns would certainly have been hard work, and carrying out these operations on a ship that might be rolling and pitching would have provided ample opportunity for these sorts of changes. He had very bad teeth, many of which he had lost during his life.

THE PURSER

A third skeleton, FCS88, was believed to be that of the purser. He was identified because he was found trapped in a compartment on the lower deck together with a chest containing a great many coins, including some which were newly minted. A group of eight shields with centrally mounted handguns were also found in this area, together with barrels that might have contained wine. Aged between 30 and 40, there was confirming evidence in his physical condition that suggested he had suffered some form of trauma in childhood, which had left him with a pronounced stoop and limited leg movement. That would have made walking difficult and certainly would never have suited him for a more active role, but would not have been a problem for the man responsible for ordering up the ship's stores and looking after the money.

THE COOK

Skeleton FCS12 was found in the hold of the ship near the galley. Male and aged between 18 and 30, he had an old scalp wound and had also suffered in the past from a fractured rib and left foot. He was wearing shoes – a sensible precaution in the galley where the ovens (see p. 55) were fuelled by a large log fire – and he carried a dagger and a comb.

All four of these characters are given prominent positions in the museum displays, and the examination of their remains has unquestionably added detail to the stories that can be told about them.

OTHER CREW MEMBERS

As well as on the full reconstruction of the figure of the archer, the technique used to model faces has been used on other skulls to produce computerised images. These images were then used to create two-dimensional representations of the faces. Some are shown clean shaven, others bearded, and with a variety of hairstyles, the choice being made to show the variety of different characters that could be seen in the Cowdray engraving. Facial reconstructions have also been made of the carpenter, an officer, a gentleman and two more archers. Altogether, it was possible to identify men who worked in six specific job categories aboard the ship: the master gunner, the cook, the carpenter, the purser, officers and four archers. The different characters are shown in their display cases together with their skulls and the artefacts associated with them.

Although the vast majority of visitors accept these displays, there are some who may find their presence offensive. A decision was thus taken not to display bones on the main deck level, and text at the entrance to the museum alerts visitors of the displays, whilst the museum plan outlines where the remains are on show.

The investigations by many experts using a variety of technologies have revealed a great deal about the

medical history of the men on board. Some suffered from rickets, a complaint associated with malnutrition in childhood; while others show signs of wounds acquired in battle, from arrow scars to broken bones. Perhaps one of the most surprising discoveries came from an investigation carried out on their teeth. As Tudor children grew up, the composition of their tooth enamel was determined to a large extent by what they ate, which varied from region to region, and on a number of other factors including local water quality and the nature of the soil in which plants were grown. Different enamel compositions have thus been successfully identified and plotted on a map of Britain. When tiny fragments were taken from 18 *Mary Rose* individuals some were identified as probably coming from the south-west of England or South Wales, but some indicated that they had not been brought up in Britain at all. They spent their early years in a much warmer climate and probably came from a region of

Respect has always been shown to those who died in the tragedy. On the opening day a wreath was laid on the waters above the wreck

southern Europe such as Spain – indeed it is known that Spanish sailors were employed on British ships at this time, but no one had expected to find large numbers on an actual English warship.

Only a small fraction of the human remains found are on display. The remainder are conserved but kept separate from the rest of the collection in the equivalent of a modern mausoleum, where they remain available for serious academic study. As with everything concerned with the human remains, applications for research need to be considered by the Human Remains Advisory Committee. It is the body that was ultimately responsible for the decision to place some of the crew's bones on display, and one cannot do better than quote its own words on the reasoning behind this. The HRAC decided that the bones were 'an integral part of the core collection' and should therefore be displayed. 'It is important that visitors are aware of the ship as a living, working entity, and that the people and tragedy underpinning the *Mary Rose* are a vital part of this story.'

The overwhelming importance of the human story was emphasised at the opening of the museum in 2013, when a launch set out into the Solent to cast a wreath onto the sea above the wreck site and a short service of remembrance was held for the crew.

7

Running the Museum

It was seven o'clock on the morning of 30 May 2013 when a day of celebrations to mark the official opening of The Mary Rose Museum began with a memorial service out on the Solent. At lunchtime a company of archers shot a volley of flaming arrows from Southsea Castle. The entrance to the museum itself was draped in a magnificent royal standard, which was later pulled clear by sea cadets to the sound of a fanfare of trumpets from the roof. The ship's bell was ceremonially carried into the museum to the traditional accompaniment of a bosun's pipe and set in place. There followed a day of Tudor jollity and, after all the ceremonials and entertainments were ended, it was time to get down to business. The museum was opened to the general public.

The visitors to the museum see only a part of a complex operation. The Trust have three other sites within the dockyard: one near the main gate contains offices; the second has the display team workshops, store, archives and photographic studio; and the third is the old Chain Test House where the conservation work continues. There are more offices in the museum building itself, and either there or somewhere among the complex of pipes and cables that snake in and around the museum, the maintenance staff are always busy. It is their job to make sure that the essential

The opening day in 2013 was marked by archers shooting burning arrows from Southsea Castle

control systems are working as they should, and to repair any faults that may occur.

Only some of the staff have direct contact with the general public. Many of those who do are there to ensure that everyone who arrives gets as rich an experience as possible from their visit. The first part of that process paradoxically involves imposing restrictions. The size of the museum was determined by the nature of the site, and it is not huge. If everyone who wanted to visit on any one day all tried to crowd in at once no one would be able to see anything, nor have any time to linger over exhibits that they find particularly fascinating. So when the museum first opened, each visitor had to book a time slot for entry. These are spaced at half-hour intervals and a maximum of 200 people are allowed to enter during any one time slot. No one has to turn up precisely

Above left: The entrance to the museum draped with a royal standard, with sea cadets waiting for the unveiling

Above right: Sailors from HMS Duncan, *the Royal Navy ship affiliated to the* Mary Rose, *carrying the ship's bell into the museum*

at the time shown: a ticket might, for example, be for 11 a.m. but entry is permitted any time between 11 a.m. and 11.30 a.m. Because visitors are advised to follow a prescribed route, one group will be well on its way by the time the next one arrives. It may sound bureaucratic, but it is an efficient way of ensuring that no one feels too overcrowded or rushed and, of course, once inside everyone can stay for as long as they like. There is no fixed exit time and in quieter periods a free-flow system can operate.

VOLUNTEERS

The people who usher the visitors around the museum are unlikely to be members of the permanent staff. The museum relies very heavily on its army of volunteers, who range in age from 16 to over 80. Many of the younger volunteers are looking for useful work experience – time spent at The Mary Rose Museum makes a useful entry on a CV – and for an older generation there is the opportunity to spend retirement years doing something that is both fascinating in itself and of real value to the community. New volunteers are given an induction course and they work alongside a more experienced volunteer for their first few sessions. There are regular updates as well as lectures they can attend to gain extra expertise. Although a lot of the work is routine – manning the front desk, acting as guides stationed at various points around the museum (it is surprising how many visitors either manage to get lost, or misplace a relative!) – there are also opportunities to do more demanding jobs.

Many of the volunteers already have particular interests and are either able to provide expert knowledge on certain types of exhibit, or give demonstrations of some of the work that was done on board. So a volunteer with a special interest in artillery, for example, would be stationed by the guns and would be available to answer questions and usually provide a wealth of information. Another volunteer might be giving demonstrations of rope work. Although a display case might give a very detailed account of the artefacts associated with one particular individual, there is an

extra bonus in having someone show exactly what those artefacts are and how they were used.

One volunteer may be found sitting behind a table covered in replicas of objects found in the surgeon's cabin. It gives people a chance to handle objects for themselves and sometimes find out some surprising facts. For example, it might seem odd to find a pepper grinder, very like one a visitor might have at home, alongside an assortment of surgical implements. We think of pepper as simply something used to flavour food, so it's fascinating to discover in the *Mary Rose*'s time that, although it was a precious commodity used to spice up an officer's meal, it was also an important medicine used in a variety of different ways: apparently equally effective as an anti-inflammatory drug, or as an anti-flatulent. Handling objects can also reveal aspects that are not obvious just by sight alone. The wooden containers for the surgeon's drugs, for instance, all have carved tops and each one is different. This was a dark ship and labels would have been difficult to read, so having an identification code that could be interpreted simply by touch had an obvious value.

The volunteers do not just learn lots of facts by rote: they often have their own expertise and bring their own personalities to the job, interacting with the visitors in their own style. It is a system very unlike that which

was once found all too often in visitor attractions, when visitors were shepherded round and given set speeches. Here it's up to individual visitors: if they want to stop and chat to volunteers or see a demonstration they can, or they can simply walk on past. It's a very natural form of communication that works because the volunteers are so obviously enthusiastic about what they do. Some dress up in Tudor costumes for the occasion; others don't. There is no compulsion to do so.

Above: A costumed volunteer explaining to visitors how the surgeon's tools were used with reproductions of artefacts from the collection

Left: Visitors beside the master gunner's display case

VISITORS

The museum tries to provide a service for as many different types of visitor as possible, with guide maps available in a variety of different languages. Individuals and family groups who turn up to enjoy a day out are also not the only visitors to the museum. The museum provides a valuable educational resource for the community, and school visits are an important part of the museum's role. As well as accepting group bookings to look round the museum, schools are offered workshops in the special education pavilion at the opposite side of the building from the main entrance. As well as a schoolroom there is a science laboratory to engage the groups. Primary schoolchildren in particular have a lot of fun while they learn. They get to dress up in Tudor costumes and play different roles; making up a gun crew or taking on a job as the navigator's apprentice. At the same time, children learn a lot across many different disciplines, whether looking at skeletons and finding out about anatomy or testing their mathematical skills as they try to plot a course across a chart.

Older age groups get far more intensive and specific courses. Some are aimed at students of Tudor history, others at science students. They get to see behind the scenes to find out about conservation and there are also special courses for children who are thinking of careers in the museum profession or the tourist industry. These are very much hands-on courses with an opportunity to touch actual artefacts. Today we live in a multicultural society, so student notes can be made available in eight different languages.

Not everyone can get to the museum, so there is also an active outreach programme. Visits to local

schools, the local community and special needs groups can all be arranged. Trevor Sapey, the Community Engagement Officer, has thus become hugely popular with many different groups, appearing in costume and giving talks and demonstrations. These are specially adapted to meet the circumstances: serious and factual for a local history society perhaps, and much more light-hearted and entertaining for patients in a hospice. The museum can even reach communities overseas via the Skype™ network.

FINANCE

Running a major museum such as this is a complex affair, a big business that requires all the usual personnel that would be involved in any other commercial concern looking after everything from finance to publicity. It is also a very expensive place to keep going. Entrance fees alone can never cover all the costs so extra revenue sources are needed. Apart from sponsorship by companies and local authorities, individuals can also contribute. They can become Friends of the Museum at a modest level or Patrons or, for those who want to make very large donations, they can join the Flag Officers' Club. But the vast majority of visitors also contribute extra to the funds through the shop and cafe.

Arriving at a rather dowdy souvenir shop stocked with tatty, off-the-peg goods can easily take the edge off a successful museum visit. A survey showed that Mary Rose Museum visitors wanted goods of high quality and ones specially made for the museum. So the shop itself had to be as well designed as every other part of the building, and the Trust was also keen to use local producers. Ceramicist Emma Bridgewater designed a range of souvenirs based on the Cowdray engraving, including a tea caddy filled with tea supplied, appropriately, by the Portsmouth Tea Company. Another range of products based on 'Hatch', the carpenter's dog, came from a company in Gosport, and the t-shirts and rugby shirts with *Mary Rose* designs came from a company in nearby Petersfield. The book section has a good range of titles dealing not just with

Above: *Out in the museum, the students have a chance to learn gun drill*

Left: *Henry's heroes: pupils role-playing in the education pavilion*

Below left: *Discovering some of the artefacts for themselves; the girl in the foreground looks at one of the carpenter's planes, being held by a member of the education team*

the ship but also other aspects of Tudor and maritime history. Arriving at the shop at the end of a tour is definitely not an anti-climax.

The cafe also follows the museum's policy of using local produce and, apart from being an attractive place to stop and refresh, it also has one of the best views of any cafe in the country. There can be few that can match an outlook that includes an historic naval dockyard and one of the nation's most iconic warships, HMS *Victory*.

One place that does perhaps offer an even better view is the museum's own Bridge Balcony. This is not open to the general public, but it is possible to book evening events, ranging from a full dinner to a drinks reception, that include access to this privileged view, as well as the rest of the museum. Events provide a new venue for the local community and add to the museum's funds.

Raising money is a never-ending process, not just to cover everyday running costs, but in helping to pay for future developments, conservation and research, together with routine monitoring of the wreck site in the Solent where structural remains of the bow still lie buried.

Left: *Some of the museum staff and volunteers*

Far left and below left: *Visitors enjoying the sun in the cafe's outdoor seating area*

Below: *The museum reception area and shop*

8

Looking to the Future

Artist's impression of the interior after the hotbox has been removed and a new gallery created with an uninterrupted view of the hull

THE MUSEUM

There are not many museums that, even before opening day, lay plans to close again in just a few years' time, but that is the case with The Mary Rose Museum. If all goes according to plan, the drying of the hull should be completed at some time in 2016. Once the conservators are convinced that all the tests show that the hull is dry and that the timbers have been stabilised, the museum doors will be closed to the public, so that work can then begin on removing the ducting, demolishing the giant hotbox and dismantling the wall separating the hull from the walkways at all levels. Once that is complete, the whole hull will be clearly seen from each of the museum's galleries and central walkways. Until this point, the public has either had to view the ship through clouds of spray or peer through the windows cut in the hotbox wall. In 2016 visitors will enter the ship hall and have an uninterrupted view of the preserved hull from stem to stern, but the hull they will be looking at will no longer be quite the same as it was before.

During the original salvage operation, a good deal of timber had to be removed before the main hull could be lifted. While deck planks have already been reinstated, other items including partitions, cabins and companionways have not. Decisions are being made

A recently retrieved anchor, still undergoing conservation

over how much, if not all, of this material should be reattached to the main body of the ship. Two important items were also recovered in 2005: part of the stem post and a large anchor. Both are still undergoing conservation so it is still uncertain when they will be included in the display.

With the removal of the hotbox, the visitor will be in the same environment as the ship, with the same atmospheric conditions as the public areas, but the essential controls of temperature and humidity will need to be maintained. Visitors will have to enter and leave the display areas through airlocks: in effect almost the entire museum will become a giant display case kept under controlled conditions. All this work will involve considerable structural changes and pose new engineering problems. The work is expected to take months rather than weeks to complete. Once finished, however, the museum will offer an even more spectacular experience and the sense of being aboard a centuries-old ship will be greatly heightened. It is something everyone concerned is keenly anticipating.

CONSERVATION, ARCHAEOLOGY AND RESEARCH

The museum restructuring around the hull represents the most fundamental change that will be expected for years to come, but great museums such as this are never static. Work continues on conservation projects behind the scenes, though not at the pace of previous years. As a result, a new organisation that was set up, The Mary Rose Archaeological Services Ltd, is now able to devote more of its time and facilities to other preservation projects. It is an intrinsically valuable service that makes the best use of the specialist facilities and the hard-earned expertise of the conservators, archaeologists, technicians and mount-makers. It will also make an increasingly important contribution to the museum funds. This is work that will continue into the foreseeable future.

Although what has already been recovered and investigated has revealed a vast amount of information about the ship and its crew, there are also a great many questions still waiting to be answered. Some of these queries might remain unsolved. For example, the rudder of the ship extends to the full height of the hull, and would have been attached to a tiller. Yet the steersman would not have been out on the open deck but in an enclosed space beneath the aft castle. So he would have no view of the sea ahead and could only have responded to orders from above if some other device was attached. The most common solution at this period would have been the whipstaff, basically a form of lever extending up through to the quarterdeck that could be used to move the tiller. Was this used on the *Mary Rose*? At present there is no evidence either way, but it is always possible, if unlikely, that some might emerge during later investigations. It is just one of many unanswered questions.

One of the most exciting prospects for further research is centred on the human remains. Increasingly, refined methods for the extraction and amplification of ancient DNA might eventually make it possible to isolate crew members from the Hampshire area, or provide information on hair and eye colour. These techniques could be used to increase the count of the fairly complete skeletons and advance our knowledge

about these individuals. One of the reasons that so much care is taken to record and preserve every single artefact in as near to its original condition as possible, is that no one can tell what techniques may be available in the future: things that seem impossible today may be possible or even commonplace in years to come.

This is one of the key features of everything that has been done in creating The Mary Rose Museum. The work that has been carried out ever since the first artefact was raised has not been done just to put something on show for the present generation to enjoy; these are priceless, unique objects that will be valued for as long as there are people who care about the past and history. The work that has been done in preserving the hull of the ancient ship is not meant to last for just a few decades, but for centuries. Who knows, but these treasures may be looked at by people to whom they will seem as remote as the remains of ancient Greece seem to us. No doubt this magnificent museum will have changed, but later generations can at least be grateful to those who created it for doing their work so conscientiously and well. It is through their efforts that the past has been preserved for the future to enjoy and marvel at.

Acknowledgements

All images © The Mary Rose Trust with the following exceptions: Courtesy of The Pepys Library, Magdalene College, Cambridge: 8; Geoff Hunt PPRMSA: 20; Courtesy of Kester Keighley: 22; Photographers International John Hoffman: 23, 60; Portsmouth News: 63, 64; John Cogill: 67; The Masters and Fellows, Magdalene College, Cambridge: 74, 75; Hufton + Crow: 96, 100 right; Helen Yates: 105, 106, 108, 110, 111; Janet Myers: 112, 113; ID Group: 116.

Contributors: Simon Clabby, Christopher Dobbs, Andy Elkerton, Paul Griffiths, Alexzandra Hildred, Mark Jones, Sue Judge, Robert Lapraik, John Lippiett, Alistair Miles, Michelle Rickman and Eleanor Schofield.

AUTHOR'S NOTE

The author would like to thank everyone at The Mary Rose Museum for their help and co-operation: the book could not have been written without them. Special thanks are due to Alexzandra Hildred and Christopher Dobbs for their meticulous reading of the whole text. Any errors that remain are the author's.